Our Thanks:

Our grateful thanks to the following people who have been fantastic in supporting Cameron and his family on their journey.

Enid Moore, Darland High School

Bea Bown and Dr. Jane Williams, Open University in Wales

Dr. Angie Shier-Jones, Open University in Wales

Phil Pierce and Jackie Bateman, Prestatyn High School

Brian Graves, Maelor High School

Professor Imre Leader, Cambridge University

Kyoshi John Lynn & Mrs Lynn, John Lynn's Black Belt Academy

The Staff at John Lynn's Black Belt Academies

Dave Crew

Acknowledgements:

David Francis Photography for the cover images & design help

Denise Yates for reading the book and writing the foreword

The National Association for Gifted Children

Ruth Cassidy for checking grammar and spelling!

© **Rod & Alison Thompson 2012**

Revision 1.1

ISBN-13: 978-1470130381

ISBN-10: 1470130386

Contents

Foreword

The first time I came across Cameron was in December 2009. He had just got his A level results and the distance learning provider he had been working with contacted me for a quotation for a press release they wanted to issue to celebrate his success.

Now, as you might imagine, we come across many children in The National Association for Gifted Children who take their exams early! However, what particularly struck me about Cameron's story then, as it continues to do now, was the passion he had for his subject, Maths, and the down to earth attitude of his parents. Supportive, yes. Keen to get things right for all their children, yes absolutely. However, they are most definitely not the kind of pushy parents the tabloids love to blame for children going into meltdown over their education as the parent pushes them to make up for what they have lost on their own.

In fact, Rod and Alison have stressed all along that they just want all of their children to follow their dreams whilst at the same time making sure that they both have their feet firmly on the ground and that their social and emotional needs are in sync with their learning needs.

Therefore, when I was asked to write the foreword for this book, I was absolutely delighted.

By definition, this is a very personal story of one family's journey to understand and support their child. In spite of this, I believe that it will strike a chord with many families whose own journey has been similar or who are in the midst of trying to understand their child and how they can help support him or her.

Certainly, for some families who have never even thought that their child might be behaving as they do because they are gifted, I hope that this book will help the penny to drop.

However, for many families, the personal experiences outlined in these pages may be very different from your own. To you I would say, look at its key messages and how these can be applied. I believe that these are that the most important thing that all parents and carers can do, whether the child is gifted or talented or not, is to support their social and emotional health and well-being and to ensure that they thrive.

This accords well with our core beliefs at The National Association for Gifted Children. For us, being gifted or talented is just the beginning of a child or young person's journey. Taking that high potential, ensuring social and emotional health and throwing in aspirations, opportunities, motivation and good old hard work, will help to ensure that that child achieves what they want to in life. However, without this social and emotional well being, we would argue, all the other pieces of the jigsaw will not fall into place.

Finally, as the book so ably demonstrates, the understanding, support and love that Alison and Rod have for Cameron (and indeed all of their children) must be at the core of what makes parents the most important educators of their children that there can be.

Denise Yates

Chief Executive
The National Association for Gifted Children
http://www.nagcbritain.org.uk

Background

The authors, Rod & Alison Thompson, are the parents of Cameron Thompson, the subject of the BBC TV documentary "The Growing Pains of a Teenage Genius" and the subject of many national and international newspaper articles. Cameron has featured on BBC1, BBC3, ITV, S4C, Channel 5 and Radio Wales, as well as in the Daily Post, Western Mail, Daily Mail, Belfast Telegraph and many more. They are both keen supporters of the excellent work done by the National Association of Gifted Children.

Cameron was born in Belfast, Northern Ireland in 1997, however moved over to England when he was only 2, before finally settling in North Wales. Both of Cameron's parents were born and educated in Belfast. Cameron has 2 sisters; Emma who is profoundly disabled, and who at the age of twelve is still in nappies and is yet to speak, and finally Bethany who is a delightful little girl and can always be found with a smile on her face!

Rod Thompson originally trained as a Sound Engineer before settling in a career as a Computer Scientist whilst Alison trained as a Massage Therapist, although ultimately spent many years as a full time carer for Emma. Both hold Black Belts in Karate and are involved in teaching several evenings a week.

"The Growing Pains of A Teenage Genius" was an extremely well received documentary which followed Cameron as he struggled to "fit in" and as he moved house and then schools. The issues that it brought up have provoked much debate; indeed the day after the programme first aired Alison took part in a live televised discussion on "The Wright Stuff", on Channel 5, entitled "Can Clever Be A Curse?". Rod has also taken part in various discussions on a number of websites, forums and chat-rooms. One thing has been made abundantly clear – the public at large simply don't get gifted children and the issues surrounding them! There are many families out there with gifted children, who may or may not have Asperger's Syndrome, who don't know what to do or who are reassured to find out that there are others out there, just like them, living with same issues.

With hindsight Cameron can be recognised as having a special talent for Mathematics from the age of 4 but realisation had thoroughly struck us when he was 6 years old. Due to numerous house moves, as well as moving from an Infant to a Junior school, and once moving school because bullying issues were being ignored, Cameron went to 6 separate primary schools. While the levels of recognition for his abilities varied, none could be said to have totally succeeded.

It was not until Cameron reached High School however that the opportunities were available for him to be able to quench his thirst for the subject. When at the age of 11 a teacher suggested he should move forward at his own pace and find a level he felt comfortable with, little did they realise where that level would be!
Within the first 4 months of High School he had taken a mock GCSE Mathematics exam and gained an A Grade.
Within 8 months he had taken the GCSE Mathematics and Additional Mathematics examinations for real and gained A* grades in both.
Within 11 months he had completed the Mathematics A-Level course and started work on his degree in Mathematics.
At the age of 13 he became "Cameron Thompson Cert. Math(Open)", having gained a distinction with the Open University.
By 16 he is on course to have completed a Bachelor of Science (with honours) degree.

Whilst Cameron certainly won't be the youngest person to gain his degree, as far as we know he will be the only one to manage it whilst still at school, amongst his peers. This idea of being able to complete a degree whilst still enjoying the same lessons as others his age is a completely new approach and one that seems to be successful. We would hope that despite his unusual intellectual demands and the social issues associated with his Asperger's Syndrome, he will grow into adulthood having experienced the full enjoyment of his childhood and be a happy and successful young man.

Despite his achievements we, as his parents, consider that our responsibility is to satisfy not just our son's intellectual needs but his social and emotional needs as well. It is for this reason that we find it utterly heartbreaking when we see the tremendous failures that some parents seem to have caused by focusing solely on developing an intellectual need, leading to children who grew up too quickly, never having known what it was like to just be a child. We have also seen, quite sadly, numerous occasions where parents went out of their way to set their children apart from their peers; they were discouraged from interacting with others because "they were better than them", they were dressed up in suits and bow-ties and they were paraded around like some sort of prize winning poodle at Crufts; this kind of behaviour is nothing to do with satisfying any need that the child has but rather a selfish need on the part of the parent. The media is very quick to respond to, and report on, short term successes but is often very reluctant to report on future, long term failures.

What is it that has made Cameron stand out? Is it the level of his mathematical ability? Is it the effort he has put in to develop it? We believe that it is the latter. There are plenty of "Camerons" out there that have the ability present but through one circumstance or another have not been able to develop it in a meaningful way. Thomas Edison perhaps said it best when he said "Genius is 1% inspiration and 99% perspiration". In other words true genius is the result of hard work, rather than simply inspired flashes of insight. The author John Ruskin further noted in 1878 that "I know of no genius but the genius of hard work".

This is why we have chosen to put our thoughts and experiences in writing and present some new ways of thinking. We are not education experts, teachers or psychologists; what we put forward is our personal views based on our own experiences, on common sense advice and in what we have encountered through research.

1 Introduction

It is unfortunate that the majority of society has come to associate gifted children with always being the product of pushy parents, firmly believing that they must have very little quality of life and that they aren't allowed to pursue interests of their own or to "just be children". After all, the reasoning appears to be, children couldn't possibly enjoy academic subjects so their focus on them must be forced on to the child by their parents! Due to this negative portrayal the situation has unfortunately been created where some parents choose simply to not pursue additional support, so great is their fear of being labelled and criticised. Even if parents do recognise that their child is gifted, and go on to try and do something, they may find that their child's school hold this opinion and so very little will be done about it. This was the situation we found ourselves in several times when Cameron was in primary school, meeting with a continual insistence that teachers couldn't, and shouldn't, do any more. It has been further recognised by many in the field that children themselves have chosen to deliberately "play down" their abilities as a result of social pressures and a fear of being teased or bullied.

Based on our experience as parents of coping with a "gifted child" (whatever that means!), it is our intention to use this book to present our own thoughts, ideas and experiences. You may not agree with what we have to say, but in reading what we have written we hope to force the reader to consider the issues, perhaps viewing the situation in ways they haven't thought about before. There are no right or wrong answers in a lot of cases; there are probably as many differing official views as there are experts! Of course no two children are the same and as such all ideas need to be considered by those who have first hand knowledge of the child themselves and each solution has to be right for the child concerned. This is intended to be an accessible discussion of our journey and many of the issues surrounding it; to help inspire debate and perhaps to save others in similar situations some of the trouble that we encountered while trying to work out what we were going to do.

Remember that books don't make perfect parents. Why? Because there is no such thing, as all parents are human and are therefore bound to make mistakes. The only aim then can be for parents to do their best and to keep an open mind. Parenting is not a scientific process that can be reduced to a set of generic rules or equations.

The path that we had to take involved trying to figure how to deal with the increasing frustration that Cameron was feeling at school at the same time as figuring out how we could work with his teachers, when all we seemed to do with the school was argue, was a long and hard journey! For several years we had no support from the educational system, finding ourselves dismissed as troublemakers which left us without any idea of what to do next or where to go. Like most people, we had always thought that any education our children needed would be automatically provided and that Cameron's teachers would always be trying to get him to achieve his best. While we knew that there are schools that fail their pupils it hadn't occurred to us that school after school that were more than satisfactory, to our knowledge, would fail to see or recognise that they were failing our child.

We knew that Cameron was brilliant at Maths but it was a struggle to try and figure out what could be done when his school flatly refused to acknowledge he was able to do a lot more than just a few pages in an extra text book. On the UK Government Website (DirectGov) it states that "schools have a responsibility to meet the educational needs of all their pupils...this includes providing greater challenges in lessons and opportunities for pupils to develop potential gifts and talents." This is all very well but what does it actually mean? It's a set of good intentions but we all know where they proverbially lead! There is nothing concrete and what happens when the "greater challenges" aren't enough from the child's point of view, because they are still bored? Who chooses what form the legally obligated opportunities will take? Who decides what the educational needs of the pupils are? Who assesses whether or not the extension or enrichment work they are providing is keeping the child engaged? In our personal experience the answer to all these questions is the school, but they are also the ones who have to prove to outside agencies that they are succeeding in fulfilling their educational responsibilities. Therefore is it necessarily in their best interests to admit that they are failing to provide for a child? Is it in their best interests either to look too carefully at the situation when they might actually find out they are failing? If nobody is looking then nobody is ever going to find out what they don't want to know.

This may seem a overly cynical attitude, and perhaps it is, but sadly it is completely justified by our own personal experience and those of people we have encountered. While everyone is definitely entitled to the benefit of the doubt, and teachers are well-trained professionals, that doesn't mean that parents should totally abandon responsibility for their child's education. How did we get to a position where people rarely think to check that if a teacher tells them that something is impossible, that they are actually correct? Parents need to have the same involved interest in their child's education as they do in every other aspect of their lives. As Dr. Ernest Boyer rightly said "You can't have an island of excellence in a sea of indifference".

We wanted Cameron to remain within mainstream education to get a broad curriculum and to mix with other children his own age. At the same time we had to try and reconcile these aims with the fact that he was bored and behaving disruptively in class, with no system set up to support those children who are, at the very least, one academic year ahead of their peers in some way. This is why we feel the need to talk publicly about the issues because it is only by raising awareness, by showing people that these problems exist, and by encouraging debate, that there might be change!

There needs to be a shift in the thinking of educators, to acknowledge that there is a responsibility to look out for those at the top end of academical ability as well as the bottom, to accept that these children can turn up anywhere, including in a small Welsh seaside town! We had to fight to find suitable resources for Cameron and were fortunate enough to finally find educational professionals who were supportive when he began high school. We had to forge our own path for Cameron much of the time; we had to try and find tutors who had enough knowledge to satisfy his need to understand and courses that would keep him interested while making sure that he continued to progress in other subjects. The process for recognition and provision for Cameron's needs was such a battle, and such an unnecessary one, that we want to prevent others having to go through that as much as is possible.

Sadly there are some parents who choose to use the label "gifted" far too quickly and without justification. There can be many reasons for this, such as the stereotypical pushy parents, misleading media information and even just a lack of clarity on the definition of the term. The UK Government website (DirectGov) defines it as, "'gifted' learners are those who have abilities in one or more academic subjects, like Maths and English" but even this is vague. How good does a child have to be before they have enough ability to qualify as gifted? Once a child is tagged as "gifted", whether rightly or wrongly, the label is seldom challenged and for some parents this continues to propagate a mistaken belief as time passes. For those who are familiar with Simon Cowell there is an interesting question to ask; is he genuinely "nasty" when he criticises the bad singers on TV talent shows or he is forcefully putting across the truth, in the only way that will get through to people who have spent years living under a false label.

One should also consider the point that the general public's definition of gifted can sometimes be very different from that of the official one previously quoted, from DirectGov, which is purely based on academic ability. That is where the "and talented" comes into play; "'talented' learners are those who have practical skills in areas like sport, music, design or creative and performing arts" (DirectGov). However the National Association for Gifted Children takes a wider view, "Gifted individuals are those who demonstrate outstanding levels of aptitude (defined as an exceptional ability to reason and learn) or competence (documented performance or achievement in top 10% or rarer) in one or more domains.". Even within schools not all teachers have the same concept of what gifted actually constitutes, much less than within counties!

In the UK, all mainstream schools are expected keep a register which identifies their gifted and talented pupils, as part of their Annual School Census, in addition to maintaining their own internal Gifted and Talented Register or More Able and Talented Register. Any decision to place a child's name on the register should be based on proper evidence such as test scores, quality of work and the views of teachers and parents, although shockingly in the early days of developing the registers (2005), it was noted that the majority of parents were never actually consulted or even knew anything about the process! Even if a child's name were to be placed on the register, that is not to say their name would stay there; since children develop at different rates, one who developed at a faster rate may only be classed as "gifted" up until the point where their peers match their pace and stage of development. Parents should not assume that they would know if their child was on the register; in 2006 a survey conducted by the National Association for Gifted Children found that only 41% of parents knew their child was named on it. Interestingly some Gifted and Talented co-ordinators have stated that they dislike, and are embarrassed by, having to justify the inclusion or non-inclusion of children on these lists to parents. Indeed in the case of the three secondary schools that Cameron has been to, we are not aware if he has ever been listed on the register! Quite what purpose this register serves is open for debate; certainly some individual schools have been highly critical of the concept in recent years, although a national register has found favour with some universities who see it as a way to plan future provision at tertiary level.

It would be fair to say that even without pushy parents, and an unclear definition, the concept of what gifted means has come to gradually encompass larger and larger groups of children in recent years. The definition of "gifted" from 20 years ago is not the same as it is today; in fact we only need to go back just 5 years to see significant changes. To some the term "gifted" is seen as interchangeable with "bright". Even the term "prodigy" seems to have changed in its definition; to many people when they hear it they think of Einstein, Newton, Pascal or Beethoven but recent media reports have seen the term applied quite liberally to those who are even just taking any GCSEs early. Can we really conclude that the same term can be used to compare someone taking one GCSE exam early with making some of the greatest scientific discoveries of our time?

A label of "gifted" is all too often seen as a bragging tool for parents. When it comes to some parents, unfortunately, this is a valid point to make; the label can be less about providing additional support for their child and more about telling everyone they come across how their child is doing better, and achieving more, than anybody else's. Every child is unique and special; why does it have to be turned into a competition?

Society is very quick to want to attach labels to everything and everyone in the belief that having a label and category automatically guarantees future success through understanding. The same argument has been used by parents of gifted children, who assert that knowing a child is gifted allows additional support to be put in place, which can be true. However since there is no agreed definition of what that support should be, if anything, or even a steadfast definition of who qualifies, then the value of a label can be negligible and indeed can have a negative effect. There is a risk that it can put additional pressure on the child to live up to a preconceived understanding of that label whether that understanding is their own, their peers, their parents or even that of their teachers!

Gifted or not, ensuring any child is given the opportunities to fulfil their potential and develop into happy, successful and productive young adults is a difficult task for any parent. The fact that a child may have some unusual educational demands should not define them as a person; being successful in life involves more than just specific areas of gifting. It requires many other skills and attitudes to come together in the right way.

It should be pointed out at this juncture that all throughout this book the word "gifted" tends to be used to refer to the more tangible gifts and talents that children may have; the kinds that pass exams or win competitions and/or trophies. This should not be taken to mean that we consider other forms of giftedness as worthless in any way whatsoever. In recent years psychologists have done extensive research into ways of identifying children who have a high degree of emotional intelligence (referred to as EQ). Children with a high EQ often demonstrate great empathy, understanding and compassion for others and tend to be very insightful about the world around them but this talent is not one that enables them to pass school exams! Unfortunately at this time much still needs to be learned in the area of EQ and currently there are no systems or processes in place to develop this in those for whom it comes naturally.

2 Intelligent, Gifted or Prodigy?

Before any talk of giftedness can begin we need to pause for a moment and think about what actually is giftedness? What do the terms "prodigy", "genius", "gifted" or "talented" really mean for the children concerned? Unfortunately there is no universally accepted definition of giftedness. Quite what it means is often fluid and changes depending on the context and physical setting in which it is used. For some, "giftedness" refers to performance, to others it is more about potential (for example a high IQ).

You may hear the refrain "everyone is gifted in their own way" but where did this notion come from; we are all different despite the fact that there are those who attempt to make us all the same. This would imply that there are never any winners or losers. By this measure then everyone is mediocre and quite frankly that is not the way the world works; there are always successes and failures and people who are better at something than others around them. The Pulitzer prize winner and noted American intellectual Walter Lipmann said that "When everyone thinks alike, no one thinks very much". This issue has even reached Disney/Pixar films, with one character saying, "Everyone's special..." to which the reply given is, "Which is another way of saying no one is." (The Incredibles, 2004) and the film deals with how people are often expected by society to do their best but also expected to not stand out from the crowd! It's impossible to do both! Everyone has something that they are good at but this could be in an academic area, or a musical talent or something as intangible as empathy for others. These aren't gifts that will pass you an exam, but where would charities be without people who had them? It is the various uses of the word "gifted" that confuse the issue as part of a constant need to "reaffirm self-worth".

Let's consider a fictitious example of an 7 year old boy called "Billy". Billy enjoys doing Maths and his parents are keen for him to do well in the subject. Billy's parents believe that much of what children are exposed to in this day and age is a bad influence and a waste of time and they don't want him watching TV, playing computer games or using the Internet. Instead, Billy's parents have him do 2-3 hours Maths every night in front of a Maths text book and more at weekends. Although he struggles to understand at times, he is able, through sheer persistence, to work his way through the material, and by the age of 11 is ready to take his GCSE examination early.

Let us now consider a second fictitious 7 year old boy who we will call "John". Like Billy, John also enjoys Maths. Whenever he can, John is at the library reading books on Maths. Rather than play computer games he would rather download Maths puzzles from the Internet. In school he is always asking questions in Maths class. It is not enough to be told how to do something; he wants to explore how and why. John only needs to be told something once; he remembers every mathematical formula he is shown and is able to relate them to each other. He is able to work out the answers to questions instinctively and just sees them in his head, even though sometimes he doesn't always know why something is why it is. At the age of 11 he looks at a GCSE Maths paper for fun and gets the highest grade. From this experience he then asks his parents to allow him to sit his Maths GCSE early.

Examining both of these examples of children which one could be called "gifted"? There is no question that both children are clearly intelligent; to be able to grasp more advanced mathematical ideas at a young age is no small feat! However could one conclude that since both children are four years ahead of their peers that both are gifted. Are they?

There are are some important distinctions that should be made:
- Is Billy demonstrating a natural talent for the subject?
- Does Billy show an understanding outside of what is being taught to him from a text book?
- Is Billy showing evidence of independent thinking in relation to his studies?

Arguably the best definition we've seen is this: **"Giftedness is a natural ability significantly higher than would be expected to be seen in a peer. It is different from a skill in that skills are learnt or acquired behaviours; rather the gifted child demonstrates an innate personal aptitude that cannot be acquired through personal effort alone"**. This is not the same concept as being intelligent or "bright". In considering this definition, and applying it to the performance versus potential debate, it seems clear that giftedness can only apply to performance. Without any evidence based on performance you cannot predict whether or not someone will have that personal aptitude referred to above.

Remember the important point that was made earlier; do not overvalue the natural ability and undervalue the contribution that hard work and persistence makes. 1% inspiration, 99% perspiration. Achievement still requires effort.

Billy is intelligent and is achieving through persistent application but when presented with a challenge that doesn't fall within the strict confines of the material which he has learnt, is he capable of solving it? Can he use the knowledge that he has and apply it in a different way? He is capable of the rote learning of advanced material but does he have a natural ability to take it out of context or an ability to apply that knowledge in different circumstances?

Let's take our analogy a little further and consider Freda. Like John, Freda enjoys the same sort of Maths puzzles and has had the same opportunities available to her. For the first several years of school she was highly successful in Maths. All throughout her early school years she got perfect scores in Maths tests and always finished the set work in class ahead of the other pupils. Sometimes she would be allowed to share a textbook of extension work with another pupil who had also finished early as there weren't enough available for one each. Often though she was given a completely different, non-Maths activity, as a reward. She initially adored school and had been desperate to go every morning.

Now however Freda is about to start High School and the situation has dramatically changed. She is frequently disruptive in class; she doesn't listen to the teacher's explanations and often fails to complete work because she simply isn't focused. Freda's teachers despair of getting her to achieve her potential and to stop misbehaving to get the other pupils' attention, while her parents have trouble getting her to go into school each morning.

Would it ever cross anyone's mind to suggest that perhaps Freda was a gifted Mathematician?

Freda had been an enthusiastic pupil. Rewarding her for her achievements was, of course, essential but it didn't provide her with any further challenge or any further stimulation. As Freda was always obliged to stick to the pace of her classmates she became increasingly dissatisfied and bored. There was no longer any challenge. She slowly became disenchanted with school, seeing it as too easy. No child likes to be fed up and ignored, surrounded by their classmates and Freda started misbehaving to try to get some attention. This has gradually spread across her other subjects, and has become her general behaviour throughout the school day. Slowly but surely, Freda is failing at school. She has become disaffected and uninterested.

If someone had given Freda encouragement and extra material in Maths early on to help keep her mind stimulated then she could have remained engaged with school and the process of learning. At the very least Freda is "bright", perhaps she is "gifted". However without further support to encourage and nurture her abilities, they have failed to develop. Perhaps the central difference between Freda and John is that John encountered teachers who were willing to spend time answering his questions and motivated to provide him with additional learning opportunities, which helped to encourage his intellectual development. Freda's natural ability for Maths has been steadily undeveloped and is sadly being wasted.

There is a current tendency in education to pursue variations on a "one size fits all" policy. Children are split into ability groups but only within their own age group. However within any one academic year there are many and varied abilities represented. There are also many areas where children will require assistance because they struggle or need encouragement where they excel. To assist those who excel, it has now become policy in the UK school system to identify approximately the top 10% of the ability range and treat these "Gifted and Talented" children as a unified group.

This of course assumes that children are able to be adequately identified in the first place. Depending on when within their school career such a determination is made, a child may simply slip through the net. After all throughout the entirety of primary school, by both teachers and Special Educational Needs Co-ordinators, it was denied that Cameron was Gifted. By the end of primary school he was, if anything, viewed as good at Maths but becoming increasingly badly behaved. Within a few months of starting high school he had shot straight through gifted to "genius"! Whatever signs the school staff had had in mind they clearly didn't see in Cameron, so his abilities weren't recognised. I am sure John would be identified as "Gifted and Talented" but would Freda?

Even with identification, where did this notion come from that suddenly all gifted children are identical in their needs? Choosing a top 10% is clearly an acceptance that there are children who have a greater natural ability than most others of their age and have different needs if they are to fulfil their potential. So how exactly did we get to this idea that simply devising a curriculum for a stereotypical gifted child would satisfy the needs of the entire group? Assuming that all gifted children are completely alike in their abilities and needs is unrealistic. Even amongst "gifted and talented" children there are a wide range of abilities. Few gifted children are universally gifted in all areas. In fact in some areas they may be behind the majority of their peers. Gifted children can also vary from being slightly ahead of their peer group in the areas they are gifted in, to being five or more years ahead in their areas of higher aptitude.

This "cookie cutter" approach creates its own set of difficulties both with intellectual and social development, as some children find areas of the "Gifted and Talented" provision easy while struggling in others. Children who still aren't finding proper stimulation provided by the additional provision may become disenchanted with school over this new failure. Equally as children, gifted children have various different social needs but also their giftedness can set them apart from others. This is not to say that if they weren't part of this separate group that the situation would suddenly change. Being especially skilled in any one area automatically makes a child slightly different, at an age where differences can be leapt on for as ammunition for the bully. The degree to which this happens, and affects children, varies from child to child.

It would be very short-sighted to restrict any description of "gifted" to purely the academic. There are those who are gifted in the areas of dance, sport or music which the educational establishment is often not entirely equipped to deal with, leaving it often to the efforts and initiative of parents and coaches to help guide them to achieving their potential. There can equally be the problem that what a school is willing or capable of providing is insufficient. For example it may be decided that a musically gifted child should receive music tuition but what they actually receive is 30 minutes of time a week, which is shared with 5 other children! How much benefit will there be, despite the fact that, on paper, the child's needs are being met?

Unfortunately society at large frequently regards children with an academic gifting differently. That is not to say by any means that parents of children gifted in non-academic subjects don't also garner criticism. In fact there are gifts that are viewed by society as more acceptable for children to spend large quantities of time pursuing and perfecting. This especially applies to sporting interests such as football and musical interests such as singing. In other words currently fashionable activities which have a certain social status and value. However there appears to be a decided bias that any child who spends time pursuing academic interests to a level beyond that of their peers must be doing so reluctantly that wouldn't be applied to a child who spent two hours every day improving their football skills. The children themselves often can become derided as "geeks" or "nerds" by their social peers. Again if they were gifted in something more fashionable then there may well be envy, but it is unlikely that there would be the same level of derision.

Within each school a number of students are identified as gifted and talented from that community. However what is to say that the children who are gifted and talented within a specific school are gifted and talented in the community at large. In a school that is more selective regarding their intake then the group is likely to be different in composition from that chosen, for example, from the small intake of a rural school. This leads to exclusions of children in one situation who would be included in another. The 10% figure referenced previously is also a loose guideline. It differs depending on school policy and definition of "gifted and talented" to the point where the percentage can vary so widely, that the figure can reach as high as 25%. This means that a child who would qualify under one school's policy for their "Gifted and Talented" programme wouldn't qualify under another school's. It is completely impossible to ascertain how many children may be missed by these particular versions of the postcode lottery.

Terminology is changing all the time. Even when it remains static the same phrases can have different meanings for different people or change their meaning over time! Currently the term used is, "Gifted and Talented" whereas before it was, "Able and talented". "Gifted" and "prodigy" are often used as interchangeable terms while "able", "bright", "clever", "smart" and "intelligent" are also often interchangeable with each other, but in some areas "able" is only used to those children who we are referring to in this book as "gifted". "Gifted" as a term has now been expanded to be a term which encompasses a much larger group of people. It has now become synonymous with any child who is achieving at a higher level in a certain area or areas than their peers. This leads us to another area of contention; must children who are labelled gifted be gifted in more than one area? There are some who would insist that children need to demonstrate a certain degree of academic proficiency across the board to qualify as gifted.

When does gifted become labelled as prodigy or genius? The media is very quick to attach such labels to children because of how impressive they sound in headlines and generally such labels should be taken with a pinch of salt; Cameron was labelled "Prodigy" by the media for being about to take a GCSE in Maths at 11 which seemed somewhat premature! On the whole though a prodigy is considered to be someone who is at the highest level of gifted. They master at an early age skills that are far beyond their level of maturity. A "genius" is a person with an exceptional intellect or ability and isn't an age dependent concept. This can cause the dividing line in children to be often somewhat blurred, apart from in some exceptional cases.

3 Identifying Giftedness

Many parents struggle to answer the question about whether or not their child is gifted. They could possibly be worried that they will be seen as determined that their child has to be better than everyone else's, or that they are biased because they are the child's parents. Not surprisingly it is a difficult question to answer because ultimately all children, gifted or not, are unique individuals with their own areas of strength and their own little quirks of personality. However there are certain traits that can be indicators. These traits by themselves are not a definitive answer by any means, but should certainly cause questions to be asked. Neither should it be expected that all gifted children will have all of these traits. However a gifted child will generally display most of them.

Often the first time parents have cause to be considering giftedness is when evidence is seen of ability that is felt to be beyond what their child should be capable of at their age. For example a child may start reading early, they may have a detailed vocabulary, they may exhibit an excellent memory or they may relate well, or even better, to adults than their peers. The awareness that there is something slightly different about a child can take a while to come together. This is because one trait or success all by itself isn't enough to attract attention or to make a child gifted.

Looking back it is easy to see signs of Cameron being gifted from very early in his school career, but it was an accumulation of a number of events that led us to decide that something needed to be done. This is how it should be, as trying to force a child to be gifted when they aren't, will not magically give them some sort of advantage. There are some parents who are completely driven to justify their children being better than everyone else's! Again it should be said that childhood is not a competitive sport, with a high achieving education as a prize for the winner! Most parents believe that their children are special, which is as it should be, but that doesn't mean that they have to be the best and that all other children's achievements are worthless. The vitriol that some, supposedly adult, parents pour on the intelligence and efforts of little boys and girls can be both utterly appalling and completely breath-taking in the worst way. These ambitious parents are probably completely surprised if their children end up developing a distorted view of their own importance in the world!

For first time parents, or parents of only children, it can be difficult to know what "normal" is in terms of child development with little or no basis for comparison. The milestones in books and pamphlets are listed as approximates because all children develop at different rates. Normally the most emphasised point in developmental guidelines is the point at which parents should seek medical advice in case there is a reason why a development stage hasn't yet been achieved. It should be noted that sadly health professionals don't necessarily take action straight away in the event of failure to meet targets; on a personal note Emma was a couple of months away from being 2 years old, not saying a word and banging her head off walls and we were told to ignore it and wait for her next official developmental check-up! The fact that Cameron was our first child and that Emma, our second, from 18 months old started to dramatically fail to achieve developmental targets meant that, for us, there was no way to compare sibling development for some years.

Even for families with multiple children it is an important consideration that giftedness is typically hereditary and therefore every child may appear to be "normal" when in actuality every one of the children is exhibiting signs of "giftedness". They are also all raised in roughly the same environment with the same opportunities until they start going to school, where they can be compared to their peers in a more standardised situation. For these reasons it is well worth looking at average developmental milestones and then comparing a child's development to what is considered the norm, while still keeping in mind that these milestone figures are averages. Therefore "normal" still covers a range and most children do indeed reach their milestones at approximately the right time, with some deviation still being considered perfectly normal. In the case of gifted children though, these milestones can be reached weeks, months and even years earlier than the typically expected time.

For example consider the following typical examples of milestones:

At three months can my child lift and turn their head, can they hold a rattle, do they smile, can they make eye contact?

At six months do they reach for and hold objects, do they open their mouth for a spoon, can they recognise familiar faces?

At twelve months can they drink from a cup (with some assistance), can they grasp small objects, can they sit unsupported?

At eighteen months can they turn the pages in a book, can they recognise themselves in a mirror, can they sort objects by shape and colour?

At two years can they feed themselves with a spoon, can they build towers of blocks, can they follow directions, do they have a vocabulary of several hundred words?

Language ability is a particularly common feature found in gifted children; typically children tend to talk earlier, have a larger vocabulary and use longer sentences. They are also slightly unusual in that gifted children prefer to talk to adults rather than other children and can have a quirky, especially for a child, and rather mature sense of humour and master irony and sarcasm a lot earlier than their peers. This risks friction as adults may appreciate their humour but other children their own age may not grasp it. Cameron's mannerisms were the source of comment from an early age, as he often came out with surprisingly mature statements for such a young child, to say nothing of the vocabulary that he used to make them. He picked up new words constantly and then went on to use them correctly. Sadly none of this helped make it easy for him to fit in at primary school.

A common feature with many (though not all gifted children) is hypersensitivity. This can apply to all senses – to smell, to touch, to sound etc. and/or it can have an emotional impact meaning that the child may be emotionally "fragile", having their feelings hurt very easily, which can be coupled with a tendency to be emotionally intense anyway. The problem with gifted children having their feelings hurt easily is that they already stand out from the other children by virtue of being gifted. Sensitivity increases the odds of their being teased, which they may react to more than most other children, meaning they are more likely to be teased again because they are guaranteed to spectacularly respond. The non-emotional sensitivities can take many forms from fear of the sound of balloons being burst to being bothered by labels on clothes. Cameron is obsessed with soft textures especially when he is trying to relax, upset or unwell.

Another common feature of gifted children is their strong ethical sense. They are often morally sensitive, very concerned with fairness, have mature judgement for their age and are inclined to question authority. This questioning means that they don't always automatically respect adults just because they are older; in common with many adults their respect has to be earned. Gifted children with their attitude to authority and fairness will often want to logically reason through why exactly they should do something. As a parent this can make life interesting to the point where we have developed a system with Cameron that we often offer a brief explanation of why we've made a decision, so that he can try and understand why. This saves everyone a lot of time and aggravation in the long run! It can be somewhat frustrating to have a small child who wants to debate even the most basic decisions, with just being told to take a coat to school turning into an unexpected discussion of recent weather patterns! In contrast gifted children can be very upset by others not sticking to rules, which can cause friction as other children can enjoy pushing their boundaries. Despite this, they don't automatically enjoy being used as an example or being given extra responsibility, which can draw unwanted attention, even though they may appear to be more mature than their peers.

Other traits are a keen sense of observation, an excellent memory and tremendous perseverance when they are interested in something. An example would be the day Cameron announced, as the family walked past an indoor playground, that over 2 years before he had been told that we would take him there sometime! If it is a subject that interests him then he applies his fantastic memory to it, which means that he knows off by heart anything he really likes; from Monty Python songs to complicated Maths formulae seen only once! His peers all watch Monty Python, and can generally quote lines at each other, but one of his friends asked us recently why exactly Cameron would bother to learn all the words of, "Always Look on the Bright Side of Life"! This doesn't mean though that there is any particular ability among gifted children for following instructions because if something more interesting comes along in the meantime a gifted child, even more than any other, can become totally distracted.

Educational Psychology

Any form of formal assessment into a child's giftedness is the territory of an Educational Psychologist. They address the educational, emotional, social, and behavioural challenges of children and adults. Educational Psychologists are applied psychologists working both within the educational system and in the community with psychological and educational assessment skills. They also use intervention techniques and methods for helping children and young people who are experiencing difficulties in learning or social adjustment. Of course going down a formal route is certainly by no means a requirement, but there are plenty of good reasons why obtaining a formal identification is invaluable.

An Educational Psychologist is particularly skilled at identifying a child's cognitive abilities and in recommending strategies which can aid in setting provision for future educational placements. They work with children and young people individually, or in groups, applying psychological knowledge and skills in a variety of different ways and strategies. Educational psychologists address problems to help promote a child's development, achievement and welfare needs and work with a wide range of other professionals and the education authorities. That said it should be noted that a number of parents have reported that schools have been reluctant to even look at such reports. In the case of private assessments this can be because the education authority and their educational psychologists don't believe that the test was appropriate, or sees the recommendations in it as unrealistic and unworkable.

A Psychologist can also be a vital source of help in looking at behavioural issues not just in school but at home as well, with the ability to advise about child development, learning, emotional well-being and behaviour and offer training on appropriate strategies. For parents it can be a difficult determination to make if their child is simply going through a phase or if there is a genuine issue which would benefit from professional assistance. All children are bound to go through difficult periods of adjustment which invariably are reflected in negative behaviour.

Whilst a Psychologist will assess ability and potential using a standard IQ test (for example the WISC IV), their evaluation provides more feedback than just a single number; they are able to assess the way a child is able to process and evaluate information as well as highlighting any particular areas of concern.

Getting to see an Educational Psychologist can be somewhat hit or miss depending on the Local Authority involved. Frequently the support of the school is needed which can cause problems; often parents are looking for a diagnosis to be able to lever additional support from the school, so they are unlikely to support this. It is possible to see someone privately after self-referral and, although this can be expensive, it is not necessarily prohibitively so. It may be that you are fortunate enough to have the service offered to you; this was the case when Cameron completed his CAT test at the age of 11. It should be noted though that there is no legal obligation on any Local Authority to assess a child simply on the basis of giftedness alone, although that is not to say that they won't.

Quite what form any assessment will take can often vary considerably. In some cases the assessment may be done at your home. The key thing is to ensure that there is a good working relationship between the family and the psychologist; without it the outcome can be affected. For the child being assessed, being put in front of a professional for a battery of tests can be quite a threatening and stressful experience. A good psychologist needs to be able to put them at their ease and get the best from them during the testing and evaluation process.

It should be remembered however that even with a label of "gifted", different Psychologists advocate different approaches. Some openly discourage any form of acceleration at all whilst others consider it an essential tool to future success. For this reason it is worth doing some background research to see if this person has a particular interest in gifted children to judge what their views typically are and what particular bias they may bring to the table.

IQ Testing

To many people making a determination of academic giftedness is simply a case of having a child take an IQ test. IQ stands for Intelligence Quotient but this is not the same as intelligence. IQ measures one particular specialised area of intelligence, but isn't capable of measuring a person's general intelligence, nor does it judge how someone is going to use the level of IQ that they have. It can't tell whether someone is going to study or make any effort to learn. Another point is that some children, and adults for that matter, don't score well in tests because they get extremely stressed so a lower score may not actually be very accurate as regards their actual IQ.

Although it might be convenient if it was that easy, measuring someone's intelligence is nowhere near that straightforward! Whilst IQ tests are certainly an invaluable diagnostic tool, great care should be taken in their administration. Many parents resort to delivering an IQ test downloaded from the Internet and, in many cases, the results should be taken with a pinch of salt. There isn't a burden of proof imposed by any form of official body on those who upload these tests to assert how effective they are before they put them on the Internet. This is to say nothing of the fact that different tests are appropriate for different age groups and different individuals' needs.

Professionals recommend that the optimum time for testing is between the ages of 5 and 9. The minimum is said to be the age where a child can be judged to most likely have developed sufficient concentration and be predictable enough to be tested. After all this is the age at which generally children are assessed to be ready to start formal education. The upper age limit is because after this age the chances of it being inaccurate increase dramatically for a number of reasons. One of these is the risk of a child's sense of perfectionism interfering as they became stressed by their need to get a perfect score. Another is that the risk of a child's result being restricted by them hitting the "test ceiling" in any IQ or ability test they take becomes greater. The test ceiling is the upper level of achievement that can be scored on any specific test, meaning that regardless of whether or not a child should be scoring higher, that is the best they can do. The problem with a test ceiling of, for example, 115, is that there is no way to tell if that is actually a child's IQ, or if they could have actually done better if it had been possible with that test. Another type of test ceiling is that if 3 questions are answered wrongly by the child then the test is stopped. This only functions if the child doesn't run out of questions before they get 3 in a row wrong!

It must be appreciated that IQ scores for children are only relative to children of a similar age. That is, a child of a certain age does not do as well on the tests as an older child or an adult who has the same IQ as them. But relative to children of a similar age, and this applies to adults as well, they do just as well as someone of the same age who has the same level of IQ. However if a gifted child has reached the stage where they are no longer engaged with school, is there any guarantee that they will score high? They might be capable of being considerably more advanced than their peers but that doesn't mean that they will!

There is a great deal of misunderstanding about what an IQ test is or means.

One of the most common myths is that IQ is a measure of intelligence. This is not entirely true; a person is said to have a high degree of intelligence if they can quickly adapt to new surroundings and act according to the immediate demands of the new situation. If that person is successful in overcoming all the hurdles they encounter, and in the process can acquire some specialised knowledge from that experience that they are able to use again in the future, then they are declared an intelligent person. In fact one definition of intelligence is, "The ability to acquire and apply knowledge and skills". By this definition intelligence is a relative term and as such it cannot be measured. The 20th century has contained an on-going debate about how many different types of intelligence there are and even whether or not they are linked or if they are independent of one another.

In the late 1990's Howard Gardner proposed the notion that intelligence is not in fact a single entity but rather there are "multiple intelligences". For example he considered that there are verbal, mathematical, visual, naturalist, musical, physical, interpersonal and intra-personal intelligences; each having their own particular strengths and characteristics. There are some in education who would argue that Howard Gardner has successfully challenged the concept that intelligence hangs together in a single structured whole but rather a child may be at different stages within each specific intelligence; for example a child may be advanced in visual intelligence but less so in physical intelligence.

In a published report written in 1993, Gardner stated "In the heyday of the psychometric and behaviourist eras, it was generally believed that intelligence was a single entity that was inherited; and that human beings - initially a blank slate - could be trained to learn anything, provided that it was presented in an appropriate way. Nowadays an increasing number of researchers believe precisely the opposite; that there exists a multitude of intelligences, quite independent of each other; that each intelligence has its own strengths and constraints; that the mind is far from unencumbered at birth; and that it is unexpectedly difficult to teach things that go against early 'naive' theories of that challenge the natural lines of force within an intelligence and its matching domains.".

Another definition of intelligence is, "the ability to learn about, learn from, understand, and interact with one's environment". This is another demonstration of how intelligence is firstly not a clear cut, easily defined and agreed upon concept and secondly that it is made up of at least several different components; IQ on the other hand is a "measure of relative intelligence" which is determined by a single or a set of standardised tests, which are relatively inflexible and measures learned skills not an individual's native, or natural, intelligence.

The second most common myth that many people have is that the IQ of a person is a static measurement, that it never changes. This can be quite a damaging perception as people who are tagged with a low IQ, for example as a result of poor education or lack of educational opportunities before they were tested, can have this low intelligence label follow them for the rest of their lives. It is especially cruel for someone to be judged on an IQ that is low for these reasons because the result says absolutely nothing about their intellectual limits or about what they are capable of achieving. IQ is in fact a ratio, so as someone learns the number earned can and will change, perhaps even drastically, and there have been many studies that have demonstrated this.

The inventor of the IQ test, French psychologist, Alfred Binet, didn't believe that intelligence was a fixed, measurable value. Along with Theodore Simon, he created the first test in 1905 with his main aim being to identify children who needed extra help to cope with a standard school curriculum. In other words he was using a test to find special needs children, who would get a low score, and this would allow them to be given the focus they needed to improve what they were capable of achieving; to allow them to improve what score they could get. It was a German psychologist, William Stern, who referred to it as testing the Intelligenz-Quotient, or IQ. Using it to establish whether or not an individual is gifted is a slight, but significant, shift in emphasis from the original purpose.

Another problem when using an IQ test as a deciding factor of whether or not a child is gifted is the inherent risk of only "identifying" children with academic gifts and missing those whose gift is in, for example, musical ability or in an athletic ability. These abilities can't be determined by an IQ test! Even with an IQ test indicating a high IQ score this is no guarantee of success; as we have mentioned before Thomas Edison famously stated "genius is 1% inspiration, 99% perspiration". A certain degree of drive and determination is essential.

Results achieved in an IQ test may vary depending on which particular test was administered and it should be recognised that there are many different forms of IQ test. The three main types are group, individual and computerised. Firstly there are group IQ tests which usually use a paper test booklet and scanned score sheets, and often give scores lower than those provided on individual tests. Secondly there are individual IQ tests which may involve several types of tasks, question and answer sessions, can have puzzle and game-like tasks included and some tasks are timed. They require a psychologist, or someone similarly qualified, to administer them, they take considerable time to undertake and then interpret, but they provide the most information about overall general aptitude. Finally there are computerised tests, which are becoming more widely available. The greatest consideration in choosing a test should be the needs of the child who is going to be taking it.

The most commonly used and recommended IQ test for gifted children in the UK seems to be the WISC-IV test – the Wechsler Intelligence Score for Children which is an individual IQ test. In 1939 David Wechsler created the Wechsler Adult Intelligence Scale, or WAIS, which he then extended downwards to create the Wechsler Intelligence Scale for Children, or WISC, which has been revised several times since to allow for the changing intelligence levels of the world's population. The point of this is that a sample of test subjects are to produce an average score of 100 on an IQ scale, and the scale and tests keep having to be revised to maintain this. The WISC-IV is the most recent revision, with the UK version being developed in 2004, and one of its features is that it doesn't require the child involved to do any reading or writing.

Modern IQ tests generate scores for several different areas which are usually language fluency, three-dimensional thinking, logical intelligence and numerical intelligence. There are many different tests available including the Stanford-Binet, WISC-R, Raven's Progressive Matrices, Cattell Culture Fair III and the Universal Non-verbal Intelligence Test, to name just a few! The variety of IQ tests available, to say nothing of the number of results that come up on an internet search, should testify to the fixation that people can have with establishing an IQ for themselves or their children.

In the end, the IQ test on its own isn't enough to say whether or not a child is gifted but can be used for this purpose by three groups of people. Firstly there are those within the education system who want a concrete measurement with which to judge a gifted child's intelligence, which of course it isn't actually capable of fulfilling, but can be a good starting point and gives a concrete figure to be put into written reports. Secondly there are those who are trying to prove the intelligence of themselves or their children to the disbelieving and finally for the many pushy, in the worst way, parents who are determined, no matter what, that their child is going to be more intelligent than anybody else's child and will do whatever it takes to prove it or make it happen. This is because they wrongly believe that an IQ score means firm proof of high intelligence, as opposed to a limited scope, ever-changing and circumstances dependant number! To quote the National Association for Gifted Children, "The more understanding of the brain's complexity we gain and the more we find out about how learning takes place, the less reliance we want to place on measures which claim to put groups of children in order - high to low." In the end though, being gifted and/or intelligent is so much more than a number!

4 Intellectual Need Is Just One Part!

Unfortunately there is no manual when it comes to raising children! What complicates matters further is the number of so-called professionals with conflicting views that all purport to provide that magical solution of guaranteeing that your children will grow up to be happy and successful. Look in any large book store and there can be found shelves of books that claim to have the answer. The continuing market for these serves to highlight just how much concern there is in the minds of both parents, and prospective parents, about giving their children the best start in life. In some cases books, experts and their systems claim to be able to give a child an "edge" or "advantage" in life, as if growing up was a competitive sport. Parenting theories even have their fashions, with much of the advice given today drastically different to that given to our parents. An obvious example is the varying opinions on whether babies should be fed on demand or to a strict schedule. If something so basic as when to feed a newborn creates such polarised opinions, then how much more will the rest of children's development?

There is a very wise saying that holds a lot of truth; "it is better to build boys and girls than to repair men and women". Perhaps what parents are most concerned with isn't getting it right so much as not getting it wrong! They look at the "mistakes" that they see being made around them, at things they disagreed with in their own upbringing or those of their friends and what they see or read in the media. Parents will also, inevitably, bring their own bias and values to the table. With so much "help" available, much of it contradicting other opinions, it is essential to filter through it and parents have to make necessary judgements about what to accept and what to ignore. People inevitably often look to those who were successful and attempt to emulate that success, to discover the key that unlocks that bright future. Perhaps that is where the case of gifted, and especially prodigy children, is slightly different. It is the "failures", or certainly the cases where errors were made, where the child became an unhappy teenager or adult, that are more inclined to gain attention when examples are given of where they are later on in their lives. There is a lot less attention to those who went on to become happy, productive and fulfilled adults.

Every parent has their own unique concerns and debates. With a gifted child there is the concern of not just providing a child with the best possible opportunities, but also with the fact that the tools and resources required are less likely to be provided easily. Education systems are by definition set up to serve a broad spectrum of individuals with the best educational background with which to progress through life. This means that the parents of children who either fall at the bottom or top of this spectrum may not find that what they see as essential for their child to successfully learn is easily accessible. For gifted children this often necessitates enquiries both inside and outside the standard education system and often parents end up taking on additional roles themselves, as there is no one else to do it!

Every child needs to be provided with whatever they need to make the most of their natural abilities and, to paraphrase the US Army slogan, to be all they can be! This is the job of all parents. However gifted children automatically have a skew in a particular direction. They are more talented, and often more comfortable, developing in that direction. That, after all, is where their strengths lie, where they can succeed and achieve the praise and rewards that come with that success. Cameron is more than happy to do Maths but is reluctant to do any form of English homework. How many children wouldn't feel happier performing an activity that they excel in and is in their comfort zone, rather than one that is difficult for them, and at which they are less proficient? However children need to be provided with broad experiences in order for them to develop into happy, balanced and fulfilled adults. A car will run for many thousands of miles as long as it is filled with fuel. After a while though problems will start if other factors haven't been considered; oil changes, tyres, spark plugs...so too with children; if the balance isn't right across all areas of development then problems can and do arise.

Intellectual Development

Every parent wants to ensure that their child is able to fulfil their academic potential. It is important to note here however the distinction between giving their child the opportunities to excel and forcing them to excel. For a parent, supporting their child's education may mean nothing more than attending the odd parent's evening, making sure they do their homework and get to school on time every morning. Hopefully though parents will choose to be more pro-actively involved in the process; in identifying the best school provision for their child, in working with their teachers to make sure that their child is both receiving, and making best use of, their educational opportunities and supporting and promoting educational opportunities at home. It is much easier, both in terms of time and commitment, to take the learning opportunities provided by the school when they are offered as a child, rather than having to return as an adult learner to gain them later in life.

In the context of a gifted child the demands placed on the parents go one step further; ensuring that the child has access to the appropriate material to stimulate their mind. Since their child may finish their work faster than their peers (because from their point of view, it is easy) this leaves the problem of what they do while waiting for everyone else to finish. Further they may well want to know in more detail about what they have been working on, all the whys and wherefores and this can be something that a teacher in charge of a class realistically, and with the best will in the world, can't dedicate the time to providing. They have an entire class of children who need their time and attention after all. Gifted children can have an extreme need to learn at a much faster pace and process a subject in much greater depth than most of their classmates. An explanation for the gifted child of why, or a development of a topic across a much broader range than is provided for their contemporaries, is what is generally meant by supplying what is known by the currently fashionable phrase of "enrichment". It is a development of a topic sideways, a fleshing out, rather than an advancement to a higher level. This is addressed in more detail later on.

If the work being provided for the class as a whole is so easy as to be uninteresting to the gifted child then other provisions are needed to keep them from becoming disaffected. If the work is too easy then children become restless and this can lead to them disrupting the rest of the class. Whilst schools can provide extension work which the "gifted and talented" children can work on while waiting for the other pupils to finish the set task, this can still prove unsatisfactory for the child as, after all, "gifted and talented" still covers a wide range of abilities in different directions. The example of the fictitious Freda who couldn't share an extension text book because she was too far ahead was taken from Cameron's personal experience; Cameron was working his way through the book that much faster than his partner with the result being the other child finally decided when they were having to flick back and forth by 6 pages that it was time to complain to the teacher! Whilst it was somewhat funny at the time, hindsight indicates that the situation was detrimental to both children. Cameron clearly was still sailing through the work, which continued to be insufficiently challenging for him, and his partner was having their learning experience disrupted both by not having proper access to their text book and by having an unsettled person sharing their desk. Psychologist Dr Peter Congden said, "Gifted children who are way ahead of classmates can become lazy and disruptive. They need to be motivated and driven."

Doing school work for years that is so easy that it requires little thought or attention from the child risks creating unrealistic expectations in their mind. Cameron got 100% in virtually all the Maths work he did. Years later when we came across some old school Maths exercise books it quickly became obvious that Cameron very, very rarely made any mistakes in this subject throughout Primary school. He came to view this as the norm. When he finally began to do Maths work that actually challenged him he was completely devastated any time he made mistakes or got marks below 95%. We have spent a lot of time over the past few years continually pointing out to Cameron that it is all right to get things wrong. He found the idea that even Maths Professors made mistakes completely astonishing! Work being too easy runs the risk of the child coming to believe that that is how it should be and ultimately they may not want to try anything more challenging which means that they run the risk of making mistakes, preferring instead to be a big fish in a small pond.

Of course just because a gifted child may have abilities in particular areas does not mean that these should be pursued to the exclusion of all others. Children should leave school with a well-rounded education. Cameron often would have happily ceased to study English because he dislikes it intensely, however he needs to be able to clearly express himself, no matter what course his life might go on to take. If his education had been narrowed down to just Maths there would be two main risks. Firstly that he would rapidly become disillusioned as what had been a fun subject he was interested in and very good at suddenly became a chore and secondly that should he ever want to diversify or change his path from purely Maths, he would either find it incredibly difficult, if not impossible, or he would find that he would have to start from scratch. It is vital to keep as many options open as possible until subject choice becomes narrowed by the necessity to specialise for GCSEs or their equivalent and then further when moving into A-Level studies. Even then, it is important to keep as many doors as possible open; for children gifted in non-academic areas a wide spread of academic subjects serves to help them reach their intellectual potential and, like with the academically gifted, leaves their future options as wide as possible. There are a number of examples in society of gifted children taking their lives in different directions. There are also several examples of famous child actors who took several years out to complete their education before returning to television, such as Jonathan Taylor Thomas who enrolled at Harvard. Very few people can truly say they knew the path that their life would take at the age of 10!

Despite the influence of peers and popular media it would be safe to say that parents impact the development of their children far more than any other source. It is the parents who choose Child Care providers, Nursery Schools and Primary Schools. It is the parents who read to and with children at home, who play games and plan outings that are both fun and stimulating and who choose whether or not to answer the flow of questions that sometimes can seem to be never ending. It is the parents that decide how much time is spent indoors or out, that organise visits to the library and regulate time spent on computers or games consoles or indeed watching television, and the content of what they view. It is the parents who influence their children's attitudes early on through their actions. If parents are interested in the world around them and encouraging, answering all of their child's questions that they know the answer to or can find out for them, sharing their child's interests and providing opportunities for new experiences then their children are much more likely to be open to new endeavours and to exploring where their strengths may lie. However even this is a balancing act. As simplistic as it may seem, it must be kept in mind that these are children and human beings that we are dealing with here; they aren't experiments or computer programs; they need time where there is no purpose except to just have fun and figure out for themselves what to do.

There is also the time when parents should step back. It isn't necessary or healthy for a child to have all their time micro-managed. Children need to learn to make choices for themselves, and these must be followed through and then to deal with the success or failure that follows. Their natural desire to make their own decisions needs to be encouraged, as does their self-discipline. One day these children will be adults leaving home who need to have the confidence and ability to make decisions for themselves. These things help greatly in intellectual development as well as boosting a child's feeling of worth and self esteem. After all, ultimately a parent's job is to make sure when they finally leave home they are as well-equipped as they could possibly be for the life ahead of them.

Social Development

Social development cannot be overlooked but it is often taken for granted that it will successfully happen. The vital lessons that children learn about getting along with the people all around them are constantly taking place throughout their school lives; children start developing socially in Nursery in, for example, learning turn taking and sharing, and continue this development until they leave school as teenagers and beyond.

Everything about a school situation is a social learning opportunity. Obviously time spent at break-times and playtimes are when much of a child's development of the skill of interacting with others takes place; this may be viewed as a very basic skill but that doesn't make it any less worthwhile. That is not to say that there are not social learning opportunities in the classroom as well; children learn to sit, work with and be in close proximity to others, to present, share and discuss ideas and to learn how to "get along" with their peers as they share everything from text books and pencils to elbow space. A school curriculum engineers many opportunities for social development by having children take part in group activities on a regular basis. These skills of working with others are all important and continue to be used as adults.

Whilst it is fair to say that school can at times be a difficult and challenging place, especially for a child who is slightly different, it is equally fair to say that it is an important vehicle for learning social skills and how to interact with peers. There is a need for children to develop the skills and rules of social interaction with those around them. Discussing the latest fad toy or TV programme may be seem frivolous and, frankly incredibly boring, to adults but it is an important chance to perfect talking about mutual interests, learning the give and take of conversation and to consider others' opinions. Having people around of their own age helps as they develop together and they move together through the same challenges of maturing into adulthood.

For any gifted child peer relationships can pose problems. Either the child may not relate well to their peers, feeling that they do not share interests or the other children may not relate well to them; either because they are resentful of their abilities or simply because they don't understand the child. The gifted child may have a more developed vocabulary and sense of humour or it might be something as basic as mostly having very different interests. However removing the child from the problem by taking them out of the standard school system, for example moving them to home-schooling, doesn't mean that they won't have to deal at some stage with the fact that they can achieve what others can't. They have to make a choice about whether they are going to accept who they are and carry on regardless or whether they are going to try and hide their light under a bushel in an attempt to fit in better. Is it not better though that children learn to deal with others' impressions of them at an early age, rather than first encountering it in their teens or early adult life?

It does mean that friendships can be problematic and school can ultimately be a lonely and isolated place; sometimes gifted children can be viewed as "arrogant" simply because their ability doesn't match their chronological age. Intellectual development beyond what is expected for their age can make their communication with their peers seem slightly odd, especially if they are at all socially immature. For this reason some gifted children feel considerably more comfortable with those older than them, but unfortunately older children tend to dislike, and therefore avoid, mixing with younger ones. In quite a few schools such interaction is discouraged, by separate playing areas or times, for this reason. Cameron had difficulties at one primary school partly due to his insistence on trying to play with children who were several years older than him.

The typical refrain on many a playground is to refer to the gifted child as a "geek" or a "nerd", both of which are terms that have been applied to Cameron on many an occasion. In fact with the advent of "social media", such taunts can continue out of school and "cyberbullying", as it has been termed, includes text messaging, Twitter and Facebook. Modern social media means that insults, teasing and vicious rumours can be exchanged without anyone actually being face-to-face. This is one of many reasons why parents need to be aware of what their children do online, and avout their online interactions. Parents and teachers need to be ever vigilant with any child who stands out from their peers, to watch for any and all forms of bullying; psychological, verbal and physical, and be quick to stamp it out immediately. Schools need to create an atmosphere where bullying is considered completely unacceptable by the student body whenever it does occur, as total elimination is sadly impossible.

Unfortunately schools cannot supervise every child for every minute of the school day so parents need to make sure their children feel they, or someone else they can trust, is approachable whenever problems occur. This is important, not only because teachers can't be all seeing in school, no matter how hard they try, or even that there will always be times when there are no adults around a child, but also because it is now possible to anonymously insult people on certain websites. It also means that parents need to take any issues their child raises seriously, as well as keeping in mind when looking for a school both what the anti-bullying policy is as well as checking with parents of pupils already there that it is paid more than lip service!

Every person is an individual with their own particular quirks, their own strengths and weaknesses; however with a gifted child their strengths may be easier to spot than with many of their peers and their weaknesses may be harder to see and may even be overlooked by most. One of Cameron's previous schools certainly encouraged his mathematical talent but didn't seem to do anything about the fact that unlike his peers he had still not learnt "joined-up" writing; it was simply overlooked because he was so good at his Maths.

One of the key things that needs to be kept in mind continually is that gifted children are more than just a set of abilities to be developed. This may seem an obvious point but from reading some of the articles written on gifted children, that doesn't always seem to be the case. These are children that are being discussed (and then teenagers) with all the uncomfortable emotions and raging hormones that involves as they make the transition to adulthood and try to figure out who they are and what their place is in the world. Whilst it is true that the situation of a gifted child in terms of what they can and/or will achieve in a specific area or areas is not typical, they still have to deal with the messy process that is "growing up" and many gifted children's intellectual development naturally outstrips their emotional and social. Although teenage years may not have been many people's favourite time of life, the social development of this period is a vital part of becoming an adult.

This is another key part of why suddenly moving a child in with others several years older than they are can have severe consequences and this issue increases as the child gets older; even a difference in age of three years becomes massive. The difference in maturity between an 11 year old and a 14 year is very different to the gap between a 15 and an 18 year old. If a 14 year old goes to university what, beyond the academic arena, do they have in common with those around him? They are surrounded by people old enough to vote, drive, smoke and drink alcohol. How many interests are they likely to share with those around them and to what degree will they fit in and feel accepted? Their academic peers don't even have to be actively hostile for there to be any problems; the simple fact is that a 14 year old has a very different way of interacting with those around them. When Cameron was taken to pick up his A-level Maths results he was surrounded by 17/18 year olds. Aside from the obvious physical differences one thing that was immediately obvious was that plans were being made all around us to celebrate/drown their sorrows, which for a large proportion of them seemed to involve a certain amount of alcohol! Cameron, standing amongst them, was getting excited about being taken to a local toy shop for some new Doctor Who figures. The social gap was abundantly clear and was proof, if any were needed, that rejecting the idea of him going part time to Sixth Form College had been the correct decision.

Strong friendships are a very important part of growing up; it is with peers that children share common experiences and it is often easier for children to discuss day to day problems with others of the same age, feeling that they understand them better than their parents who couldn't possible comprehend what they are feeling! As children grow up they begin to spend more and more time with their friends and less time with their parents and for this reason friends often have the biggest influence on a child's thinking and behaviour. This is the essence of what peer pressure is about.

Peer pressure isn't necessarily a negative concept; it can be a great motivator to do well in school, to pursue hobbies and interests or to succeed in a competitive environment. As unpleasant as it sometimes is, the negative aspects of peer relations can also be seen as an invaluable learning experience, as long as a school is on the ball should things get out of hand or start to turn physical. Although parents would like to be able to protect their children from the world, it simply isn't possible or indeed healthy. All children need to learn how to deal with the fact that life can contain unpleasant people as well as those who won't like them and who may treat them badly or even just totally ignore them. This reality needs to be faced sooner or later, coping mechanisms developed and the realities of life accepted; learning to deal with the negative reactions of others to their achievements early on, rather than suddenly encountering them as adults when their parents can no longer support or shield them to the same degree. This is an important skill for anyone to develop; there is a very wise saying that goes "the only taste some people have of success is taking a bite out of you".

As adulthood approaches children need to be able to stand on their own two feet, gradually needing less and less parental support. It is easy for parents to feel torn, fearing the natural separation that can exist; however it is important to recognise that encouraging and nurturing their independence can be a good thing, especially if parents stay involved, even if it is just from the sidelines. Children need to develop their own personalities and coping strategies, to learn to stand up for themselves and to become happy and healthy, mentally as well as physically, young adults.

Emotional Development

What does emotional development actually mean? It refers to the development of children's awareness, control of and response to their own emotions. Emotional and intellectual development combine together to help create healthy social development, the aim of which is to produce a healthy emotional state. For example an older child who, when they get upset, throws a temper tantrum due to poor emotional control and immaturity in their responses to their own feelings, will have difficulty in interactions with their peers due to their behaviour. This in turn will restrict and hinder the child's social development as other children poorly react to their "bad" behaviour.

Children achieve emotional development through both social interaction and time spent on their own. There are plenty of scenarios which challenge the emotional control of young children that fall outside the realm of involvement with others; for example how they react when a toy breaks or when their normal routine is disrupted. Parents need to encourage their children when they are successful in responding appropriately and guide them to a more fitting response on those occasions that they fall short. They need to be aware of the need to set a good example of how to respond to life's challenges and to the behaviour of others for their children to follow. "Do as I say but don't do as I do" is even more unimpressive and hollow to children's ears than it is for adults, with them learning by the example and responses of those around them.

Often emotional development requires parents to be willing to take a step back. If children are only exposed to positive emotions and shielded from ever becoming upset or disappointed then they will be poorly equipped for life's challenges when they inevitably occur. This "protection" of a child is actually damaging to their emotional well-being and leaves children with unrealistic expectations of the world around them. Everyone has observed at one time or another a child who is "spoilt" by being given everything they want. These children have learnt from their parents that their expectations will always be met and their emotional development can become stalled as they continue to use the same strategies to achieve their ends as they did when they were toddlers; namely the temper tantrum. They are then understandably unable to deal with school or peer situations where their immature responses fail to elicit the usual favourable response they have come to expect. We have encountered siblings who kicked their own parents when they failed to get their own way. This was a behaviour that their parents had inadvertently reinforced and encouraged by giving in to it on numerous occasions over an extended period. When these children then started primary school they used the same pattern of behaviour they had used with their parents, with their peers. Their parents had always given in whenever they had thrown a temper tantrum or lashed out when they didn't get their own way. They therefore thought that that was the way people were supposed to behave and react, and so did the same with their peers at school. This wasn't unreasonable behaviour for these siblings to exhibit, as it is the way they had been conditioned and taught to behave by their parents, even if it was done unknowingly. Instead these children had their social development damaged as their peers began to avoid them in favour of other classmates, which in turn restricted their emotional development as the opportunities for them to develop beyond this pattern were limited. By the time their parents realised that there was an issue the behaviour had become deeply entrenched, and needed far more work to modify than it would have required to develop healthy, constructive patterns in the first place. Perhaps parents should consider that there is actually a very good reason why giving in to bad behaviour by children and letting them have whatever they demand is referred to as being "spoilt"!

Social disagreements and friction are often beneficial with the experience that they provide, even though parents may want to smooth the social path. It can be difficult to observe children having arguments but it is generally more beneficial long term to allow them to work it out amongst themselves; having learnt another lesson in self-control and how to get along with others. Of course the exception is where the situation between the children starts to risk becoming a physical, or verbally vicious, confrontation.

As much as childhood should be a positive experience, it is also a continual preparation for adulthood where it is a complete impossibility that they will never encounter failure. Life experience teaches emotional development and it rarely does children any favours to hide real life experiences from them when they should be able to have the opportunity to learn. Emotional development encompasses children dealing with the feelings that they have about themselves and others, as well as their capabilities to be able to function in the world from a social standpoint. Developing coping strategies and self-control engender a feeling of self-confidence in a child, leaving them in a more favourable, more emotionally mature position from which to deal with the difficulties that life may throw at them.

Once again, while children need the opportunity to just be children, much of what they are constantly doing is preparing them for becoming adults. Every decision that we make for our children should, and generally does, help to develop them in one of these three areas; Intellectual, Social and Emotional Development, often in more than one of these. However if development in one area is delayed this will inevitably have some knock-on effect. All three areas need to have the opportunity for growth to give a child the best chance in life.

That brings us round to the big question – why shouldn't children go to University early? It's perfectly simple; putting children into an adult environment does not satisfy their social development or their emotional development needs. A sudden leap from being surrounded by those experiencing roughly the same level of development socially, emotionally and intellectually to being placed in an environment with those far more advanced in those areas, risks leaving them struggling. This is especially unfortunate in that it is teenagers who are sent to university early; it is in the early teenage years when children begin to feel the need to make decisions for themselves and to start being treated as the young adults they are becoming. This happens at the same time as dealing with additional stresses in their schooling and the increase in their social responsibilities that are an inevitable part of growing up. There are good reasons why this is the age when children become legally responsible for their actions, for this is the period where they are judged capable of controlling themselves and being old enough to know that their actions have consequences. Heaped on top of this automatic increase in self-responsibility is the additional stress of leaving home, friends and their normal interactions to be placed in a totally different environment where they are noticeably different from all their new "peers". As well as the unavoidable pressure to continue to succeed in the same way that got them entrance to university in the first place, they are now on totally unfamiliar social and emotional ground and in trying to successfully integrate may find themselves faced with the impossible task of having to find several years of maturity overnight.

It is a sad fact that Cameron's friendly, enquiring and open nature has repeatedly been greeted with pleased surprise when he met education professionals who already knew that he was undertaking degree studies. It is also rather concerning that the fact that we let Cameron explain what his past achievements and current studies were was considered deeply unusual with the expectation being that his parents would speak for him. That, and the fact that we only intervene when Cameron accidentally confuses others with the sometimes haphazard way he relates events or where he hasn't clearly explained himself, seems to have made us stand out from other parents encountered. We have always considered it important for Cameron to express himself and by letting him talk for himself he is being allowed to develop his social skills. Having to be halted, either momentarily for explanation, or totally so that he can be moved on to a different topic, are still development opportunities as Cameron learns and improves his conversation and social skills with his experiences.

As well as the issue of university, it is worth addressing the subject of boarding schools. Any consideration of a boarding school needs to be a joint decision between the parents and the child and much thought needs to be given as to how this will impact their emotional development through their separation from their family. Some children do well at boarding school, others don't. The option was raised once when Cameron was still in primary school and his reaction was one of complete horror. His social and emotional maturity were at a level (and still are) where the idea of being removed from his family was unthinkable for him and so this idea was promptly rejected by us. Boarding schools are a relatively closed environment. If a child isn't already socially and emotionally developed, they are likely to find it very difficult to thrive in what can be a pressure cooker situation.

The media is quick to report on children that are sent to university at a young age; they are not so quick to report on what happens next. The general public love to read these inspirational and aspirational stories about children achieving the incredible, but no-one wants to hear about children that are damaged by their ambitions and those of their parents, and of how such initial promise disintegrated and left confused and devastated young people, and their families, in its wake to try and pick up the pieces. The initial success stories inspire parents who are looking for footsteps for their children to follow in; they therefore hardly want to hear about failures, especially as many of the children involved in situations where it went badly, go on in adulthood to blame their parents for pushing them too hard and too fast, ironically destroying the very potential their parents had worked so hard to foster.

A similar argument can be used in relation to home schooling. Without getting into arguments over the relative merits of such an approach (and we are not saying that there is no place for or value in home education), parents who choose to home educate need to ensure that such children are provided with alternative avenues whereby they are able to develop their social skills. Within the typical classroom setting a child will engage in group projects and class discussions; they will learn from other pupils. Successful education needs to involve learning how to work with others; if they end up going to university they will need the skills to be able to fit into the group environment.

Physical Development

Whilst physical development isn't one of the main three areas of social, emotional and intellectual, it is an important point to bring up.

Many gifted children are more interested in mainly academic pursuits than they are in any physical or sporting interest. Of course not having an interest in football, for example, is perfectly fine but it is worth noting that whilst children may not want to engage in physical activities, frequent exercise of some sort is vital for health and well-being, both now and in the future. The British Heart Foundation have clearly stated that it is "crucial" to encourage good exercise habits in children, laying down the foundations for good health in later life. As with intellectual, social and emotional development this is a good stage to be setting good habits and attitudes for life.

Some of the long term health benefits of exercise are:

- A stronger immune system; the body's ability to fight disease is improved and children are less prone to colds, allergies, and many other diseases. Childhood inevitably includes enough illness without leaving children more vulnerable than they have to be.

- A reduction of type 2 diabetes risk by increasing insulin sensitivity and improving carbohydrate metabolism. Again setting good habits in childhood lowers the risk both in childhood and in later life.

- A lower blood pressure and an improvement in cholesterol profile, both helpful for long term health especially with the stress that a high achieving lifestyle risks bringing.

- A strengthening of the entire cardiovascular system, including the heart and lungs. This is a circular process as exercise strengthens them, which then makes it easier to exercise further!

- Children are less likely to become overweight and will have better control of their body fat. Even for adults it is a lot easier to maintain a healthy weight than it is to lose excess fat, especially as any weight-loss programme is further complicated by the fact that children's bodies still need the necessary fuel and nutrients to grow. Being overweight in childhood creates emotional and social development issues as it is frequently a source of bullying, meaning there can be difficulties in more extreme cases in keeping up with their peers when playing, and of course the well-known risk of being the last one picked for teams, which is upsetting for any child.

- Children develop stronger bones and muscle structure, which is especially important as their bodies are growing and developing at a rapid rate. Activities that impact on the body such as Martial Arts or running help strengthen bones by encouraging good bone density.

Even with short term exercise the benefits are not insignificant:

- Exercise increases the blood flow to all body tissues, including the brain; greater blood flow transports more oxygen and nutrients to the body's cells. It also improves absorption of nutrients from children's diet with the improved blood flow to the digestive system.

- Active children improve their body's ability to absorb oxygen through aerobic exercise which leaves them feeling more energised and alert. More oxygen translates into more energy!

- Increased blood flow promotes the body's transportation of the by-products of metabolism and toxins back from the cells for elimination, recycling, or further use elsewhere. As a result children who exercise feel fitter and more energetic.

- Exercise improves the function of the lymphatic system which is a vital part of the immune system, removes toxins and excess fluid from the body cells and delivers oxygen and nutrients from the blood supply to cells. The lymphatic system relies on gravity and muscle movement to function therefore the more movement, the more effective it is!

- Active children breathe better and sweat more, both of which are great ways to detoxify the body, making it function more efficiently and help it keep itself "clean."

Physical health factors aside, exercise has been shown in many studies to have a significant impact on mental health and psychological development. For example exercise has been shown to result in better memory, improved concentration, decreased anxiety, improved mood and reduced depression.

As well as exercise, physical development is as much about good diet as it is about exercise. Children who eat a variety of healthy foods feel better, more alert and are able to enjoy a better quality of life; eating a balanced diet also can prevent serious health problems in later life. Many, many books have been written on the subject of child nutrition and any mention of it here would not do the matter justice. Suffice to say it is important for parents to understand the benefits of healthy eating in physical development, psychological development and mental growth.

A study conducted in Bristol looking into the long-term health and well-being of approximately 14,000 children suggested that diets high in fat, sugar and processed foods for 3 year old's can caused a measurable reduction in IQ by the age of 8 and a half. Commenting on the study the Director of Research from the School Food Trust responded "given that around 23% of children start school either overweight or obese, it's absolutely clear that healthy choices as part of their early development will stand children in good stead – not only for keeping a healthy weight as they grow up, but as this evidence suggests, improving their ability to do well at school".

We must also consider the effect of what, and how much children drink.

High consumption of sugary drinks has been linked to development of type 2 diabetes. On the other hand drinking water on a regular basis has been found to improve concentration and physical performance as children become more easily dehydrated than adults. Just a 2% drop in a child's hydration can cause a 20% drop in their performance!

It may be beneficial to talk to the family doctor about the impact of dietary changes on behavioural issues; many children have been found to exhibit problems attributed to common food additives or even intolerance to certain foods, as opposed to allergies, which can create nausea and abdominal pain, which would badly affect anybody's mood! The latter was the case with Cameron's sister, Emma, but was done on the advice, and at the suggestion of, a health professional. It is unwise to start narrowing the diet a child receives without good reason and making sure that whatever nutritional value was provided is replaced by other means.

Child development is a balancing act of the intellectual, social, emotional and physical, often hidden within the day to day events of childhood, with skills being continuously learned. It is important to keep a child in school with those the same age as themselves for their balanced development unless there is an definitive and conclusive reason not to (and more than just accelerating education). A child needs to learn how to work with others; sporting activities and other group settings simply don't provide a forum for working with others in a collaborative intellectual way (in the same way they will be expected to do in a university or workplace situation). In a classroom environment children learn about different ethnicities, cultures, lifestyles and opinions and how to co-exist with them. They meet those with greater or lesser advantages than their own and those with greater or lesser abilities than they possess. They learn to co-exist, accept and work with those different from themselves. They acquire their social and emotional development being in that environment for five days a week, month after month, surrounded by others learning the same lessons and going through the same journey as them towards becoming adults.

5 The Big Dilemma!

Given the damaging psychological effects of hothousing and the constant need to ensure a balance between the social, emotional and intellectual needs, any question of early entry to university is simply unrealistic. No doubt there will be people happy to argue this point, but the fact remains that removing a child from the company of their peers eliminates what is ultimately one of the best resources they have in developing their social and emotional skills. These children are forced to attempt to accelerate the transition from childhood to adulthood without being able to share the experiences with their peers. Whilst they may no longer differ from those around them in terms of what they can achieve academically, they instead are set apart by their social and emotional immaturity, lack of shared interests and even their physical appearance declares their divergence from the norm.

Society today seems to be of the view that the problems associated with gifted children and their education is a modern phenomenon; that in days gone by these children coped perfectly well and it is only modern attitudes and political correctness that has created these issues. This is not the case. More than fifty years ago the Journal of Teacher Education featured an article about gifted children in which it was stated that "by this refusal to recognize special gifts, we have wasted and dissipated, driven into apathy or schizophrenia, uncounted numbers of gifted children. If they learn easily, they are penalized for being bored when they have nothing to do; if they excel in some outstanding way, they are penalized for being conspicuously better than the peer group and teachers warn the gifted child, 'Yes, you can do that; it's much more interesting than what the others are doing. But, remember, the rest of the class will dislike you for it.' Meanwhile, the parents are terrorized with behests to bring up their children to be normal happy human beings". This statement serves as a simple demonstration of just how far from a modern idea these issues are, as well as a warning over just how ineffective previous strategies have been. You would think that after five decades a solution would have been found and some kind of consensus could have been reached amongst educational professionals!

It would of course be very easy to choose to do nothing to further support a gifted child, relying solely on the intervention of the school. Such an approach relies entirely on the individual school having both the will, the time and the expertise to provide what a gifted child may need. During Cameron's primary education we were told on numerous occasions that Cameron was already being provided with enough Maths extension work to keep him stimulated, which he clearly wasn't because he was so bored that he was restless, unfocused and misbehaving in class, regardless of the subject. We were told on several different occasions by different schools that there was no possibility that Cameron had any form of Autistic Spectrum Disorder; the fact that one of the people to tell us this was a school's Special Educational Needs Co-ordinator clearly demonstrates that educational professionals are not perfect, seeing as he has now been formally diagnosed with a clear cut case of Asperger's Syndrome. Ultimately children can be so complex and challenging at times that it would be unfair to expect a teacher to be able to cope with every child they come in to contact with without further professional support. His final primary school were so determined that advancing Cameron was wrong, that it now appears that they viewed any requests to examine and assess Cameron for Asperger's Syndrome as a way to get at them, or as a way for the parents to get their own way. They were so adamant and narrow-minded in hiding issues, and trying to turn Cameron into a stereotypical young boy that they frankly ignored a lot of the issues, ultimately only admitting the scale of the problem just as he was about to move in to secondary school when presumably the view was that he would be someone else's problem.

Unfortunately in many cases schools are ill equipped to be able to deal with gifted children. That is not to say they cannot support the brighter children at the top of the class but where that ability extends outside of the year group and beyond there are few options available. This is not the fault of the individual schools; a school is expected to be all things to all people which in some ways is doomed to failure even from the start. Even a highly motivated teacher has only so much time available and a group of children with a myriad of different needs has to be able to split their time appropriately and not be seen to favour one student over another. Lack of staff or funding is often as much of a problem as lack of understanding of the need for different strategies or even, if the need is recognised, what the best course of action is to fulfil it. This is why one of the things that the National Association for Gifted Children (NAGC) is striving for is specialised advocacy for gifted children; there hasn't traditionally been a lot of work done on producing an appropriate specialised curriculum which looks to address the unique demands of the gifted child.

Recently there have been moves in many schools to appoint "Gifted and Talented Co-ordinators" or as they are also known "More Able and Talented Co-ordinators". On the whole this has to be considered a good thing; firstly it is an acknowledgement that gifted and talented children can have requirements for which provision needs to be made; secondly that having an understanding of the needs of gifted and talented children may be outside the skill set of some teachers and thirdly that the best arrangement is to have someone who can take the time to deal with whatever systems or services need to be provided and to manage any difficulties that may occur. This is very definitely a positive step; frequently it can be that case that all a teacher requires is simply the tools to assist the child in question. If the child's ability lies, for example in music, then the Co-ordinator is able to bring in a Tutor and arrange for tuition sessions. These co-ordinators are also able to put in place systems to enable teachers to recognise gifted children and, when they are recognised, to ensure that to the best of their ability are able to meet the needs. Unfortunately in practice it hasn't always worked out for the best; changes in education don't happen overnight and those appointed to the role have struggled at times with being able to meet expectations. Schools have a wide range of targets to meet already, and having yet another one imposed on them can be met with resentment. Most schools struggle as it is in coping with the tremendous demands on their time and on their budgets without having to cope with even more demands being placed upon them. Most parents are all to familiar with the begging letters coming home with their children on a regular basis looking for volunteers, additional finances or some other form of help! Knowing that something has to be provided is not the same as knowing what form it should take and how it should be implemented.

The term "special needs" is one which is freely used within education and a quick search of an encyclopedia gives the meaning of the term as "particular educational requirements resulting from learning difficulties, physical disability, or emotional and behavioural difficulties"; in other words a child who requires additional support just to be able to keep up with their peers. A considerable amount of time, resources and money has been spent on developing systems and procedures to support children in this position, and quite rightly so, but the question needs to be asked over where this definition came from why the word "special" means "difficulty"? A cursory glance at the dictionary defines the word "special" as meaning "otherwise different from what is usual"; it doesn't say "not as good as", it says "different". So why shouldn't "special needs" include those children at the top end of the scale who are ahead of their peers, who thirst for knowledge and who show a level of understanding above their years.

The more gifted a child is, the more clear cut it becomes that they do have a need for additional support and their needs are very different to most, if not all, of their classmates. Schools need to justify their performance through the grades and exam results of their pupils. Improvement of the majority of children's academic status, and that of those who were underachieving, is easily measured by exam results. Unfortunately improvements in conditions and provisions for gifted children aren't necessarily something so easily measured, which can mean there is less incentive to take action in schools where there is already pressure to show better performance, with efforts remaining concentrated in areas where there are more tangible results.

By the narrow definition of "Special Needs" as only applying to those who need support to keep up with their peers it would seem that there is an almost an unwritten notion that there is nothing "special" about the needs of gifted children; a clearly ridiculous concept. So who do schools turn to when they find that they have a pupil whose needs have progressed in certain areas beyond what they can fulfil but they still have a responsibility to educate them?

When Cameron completed his GCSE examinations in Maths and Additional Maths at the age of 11 the first obvious question we had to ask was "what next?". Although the GCSE exams had been easy for him, the dissatisfaction and boredom, with accompanying restless behaviour which had been such an issue in primary school across all subjects, had abruptly ceased. However, there was no clearly set out plan of what to do next and at the time we had just moved house into a new area some forty miles away. Cameron had no choice but to change school. Had we have been able to find a way to keep him at his current High School we would have done so; Prestatyn High School could not be praised highly enough for the support (both pastoral and academic) that they were able to give at a time when there was no official policy for Gifted and Talented set down by the Local Authority in Denbighshire.

There were three options put forward:

- Do nothing. He would stop his Maths for the time being, secure in the knowledge he had got 2 GCSEs "out of the way" early, achieved excellent Grades and didn't have to worry about Maths any more.
- Move on to take the A-Level examinations by attending the local Sixth Form College part time and the nearest High School the rest of the time. (Many schools in the current climate only operate up to age 16 and further A-Level studies and vocational training are undertaken at specialist sixth form colleges.)
- Look for a school that wouldn't necessarily be the closest school, but which would have teachers that were capable of supporting

his studies at A-Level standard without having to put him in a more mature environment.

Realistically only one of these options was ever a serious consideration. Had we chosen to force him to put a stop to his Maths, we would be taking something away from him that he enjoyed and thereby restricting his intellectual development not to mention his enjoyment of the subject. Would he therefore resume going to the same Maths classes as his peers and end up spending five academic years repeating work he had already covered? Needless to say this would be incredibly frustrating for anyone, much more so for an 11 year old.

The difference in Cameron's behaviour in high school compared to primary school alone was enough to cause us to reject the idea of dropping Maths. Cameron's final school report in primary school was a warning sign that something really needed to be done, with him getting great marks in all areas, but at the same time there were constant complaints from teachers that he was capable of more, especially if he would listen to explanations and stop mucking about in class. It should be pointed out that this report was end of year, in fact end of primary education, and was the first admission from the school that there was actually a problem. Throughout endless discussions and meetings that year both teaching staff and the Special Educational Needs Co-ordinator had denied there was any real problem, refused to address any issues or assess him for any special needs, dragged out every action that they chose to undertake and essentially implied that we were either imagining problems or just being plain awkward. Only when Cameron was on the point of leaving for high school did they admit the extent of his concentration issues; in other words at a point where it was about to be someone's else's problem and they wouldn't have to work out what action to take or undertake any work themselves, did they acknowledge there was a problem!

The significant first step for change between primary and high school was that a Cognitive Ability Test (CAT) had revealed that Cameron had a potentially exceptional ability in the "quantitative" section and this had led, in small steps, to his taking the two GCSE exams at the end of the year. This included him undertaking a mock GCSE Maths paper soon after Christmas, where he achieved an A grade. Taking action to finally allow him to use his gift and actually start to exercise his ability had completely changed his educational experience. Stopping his Maths progress would have been both damaging to the rest of his academic and intellectual development but also would have been very upsetting for Cameron. Cameron was thrilled to be learning, had loved doing the GCSE preparation work and was secure in the knowledge that he was succeeding; to halt his progress would have been emotionally devastating for him.

The second option doesn't fair much better in that whilst sending him to a Sixth Form College would satisfy an intellectual need, it would place him in an environment that would be wholly unsuitable for his level of social and emotional development at that time. Cameron had spent a limited amount of time, from January through to May, taking part in the occasional GCSE Maths class and had been fortunate that he hadn't faced any particular problems. This was probably more than partly due to the fact that it was possible to partner him with two students in that class whom he had coincidentally met previously. They had been involved in helping behind the scenes at a charity Christmas concert we had been involved in organising, and had become friends with Cameron over mutual gaming interests. However the gap between a 12 year old at school and a 17 year olds at College is far more significant than that between 11 and 16 year olds who are attending the same school even though nominally it is a five year gap. Therefore from a social and emotional development viewpoint this option was deemed unsuitable and dismissed.

Even ignoring the issues associated with his social needs, moving between two places of education would have been a logistical nightmare, not to mention the time lost during the school day that would have been given up to travelling time. Given that both would be completely separate institutions, timetabling conflicts would inevitably occur and would ultimately impact on future success in other subjects. As a part-time student it would have been even harder for Cameron to try to fit in with either his fellow College students or the other school pupils. Moving back and forth would be another cause for him to be somewhat disconnected from his peers and stand out.

It is the third option that was felt to be the best solution in that it satisfied Cameron's intellectual needs whilst at the same time ensured the environment he was in was the one best suited to him and most appropriate for his social and emotional development. He would still be in the same school community on a full time basis and the issues of transport and travel time would be eliminated.

However that is not to say that this option is not without issue. Whilst the school would be in a position to teach the A-Level materials, that did not mean it would not involve potentially putting him into a class of significantly older children. We still have the issue of timetabling constraints which would mean that in order to attend the classes, time would be sacrificed which should have been dedicated to other subjects, leaving Cameron either missing out on other subjects or trying to find time to catch up on them somehow. Given that Cameron at the time had just completed the GCSE course in a few short weeks and had already moved on to A-Level material, there was concern that forcing a pace on him that took the course over two years would again result in the same boredom we had seen before.

On the surface it would seem to be a no-win situation, that no matter what choice is made, something has to suffer if there was to be any intention of moving forward. A big part of the problem with this situation was the fact that it was an academic area that Cameron's gift was in and would therefore require some kind of formal educational structure to develop further.

If the fact that it is Maths is taken out of the problem and substituted with an interest in something else, such as computer games or football, then it would be much easier to ensure his interests were stimulated on a more casual basis. A child who enjoys computer games sits down in front of the computer and enjoys himself; he improves though repetition and through challenging his ability against others! For football a child often goes to the local park with a ball and has a kick-about! So from this it could be argued that applying such a rigid structure to his interest and talent (i.e. a strict taught classroom setting) simply because it happened to be an academic subject is potentially counter-productive. No-one goes to computer games class for their hobby so why should he go to Maths class? That said Cameron had made it quite clear that he wanted the A-Level; he had set himself a goal to achieve something and he was very much focused on that goal. He had enjoyed his GCSE work so much that he was really desperate to continue with the A-Level now that there was the possibility of more advanced learning being available. Cameron had found something that he completely excelled at, that he absolutely adored and he understandably wanted to keep going. At the same time we were unhappy with the compromises which were necessary if we took any of the initial three options that were suggested.

For this reason our thoughts led us to a fourth option; distance learning. Distance learning has been successful for many many people for a number of years, offering the structure and content of the material in question but designed in such a way that it does not disrupt everyday life. On paper this would mean that Cameron could still gain his A-Level and achieve the satisfaction that he would get from that but at his own pace and in his own time. Distance learning for children has unfairly gained an association with children being unwillingly pushed into learning for which their schools don't believe they are ready but which their parents insist on. At the end of the day distance learning is simply a tool that cannot and should not be criticised for how some would choose to use it. Realistically, what is the difference between an adult looking to improve their skill set whilst still in employment and supporting their family, and a young boy looking to learn A-Level Maths whilst still in a school setting and still being in a position to grow socially and emotionally within the appropriate environment? Used in this way distance learning is an excellent tool which gives the best possible solution in the circumstances. The search for non-traditional methods of providing gifted children with everything they need is something that the National Association for Gifted Children itself is involved in.

Following discussions with teaching staff, and of course with Cameron himself, it was felt that this was a very viable option. Since the materials he would be sent were designed to be used at a student's own pace Cameron was free to pursue his A-Level studies as slow or as fast as he chose, remembering that he had covered five years worth of Maths high school material in about three months! Further, by having this "self-taught" approach Cameron was able to study towards his A-Level whilst his peers were studying at their level, ensuring that no other subject was compromised and a broad range of interests could still be observed. He was able to go into the same classroom, he would just be studying using his own textbooks. This wasn't a situation that was unfamiliar to Cameron; after all he had spent a considerable portion of primary school Maths classes working solo on extension textbooks. All that was left for the school to do was monitor and assist when necessary, rather than teach and then, at a point where Cameron felt he was ready, to administer the mock examination and the actual examination if he was viewed to be ready. Cameron being reasonably assured of gaining a good grade was essential before he undertook any actual exams; at no point were we going to allow Cameron to be in a position to suffer a failure and any resulting embarrassment. We have come to believe that unless a child can achieve an excellent grade in an exam then they shouldn't be taking it early, as what is gained by a 6 or 7 year old getting a D or E GCSE grade? They certainly aren't in any position to move on!

Suffice to say allowing Cameron to set his own pace for the A-Level material resulted in him moving an at a very much accelerated pace and it soon became clear that the A-Level material was not sufficiently challenging to him and the old dilemma returned. Cameron had simply sailed through the A-Level material with little difficulty but now had to wait until the appropriate time of year for the exams. Further consideration had to be given to the fact that A-Level Maths is a set of six exams, each representing a different module of material and it was felt that there was too much of a risk of creating unnecessary pressure on Cameron by having him revising and thinking about so many exams simultaneously. In the second year of modern high school pupils have relatively little experience of exams and so it was decided that Cameron would follow the route of taking the first three exams to achieve his AS-Level in January and then go on to take the last three exams to complete the A-Level in May. Once again though, Cameron had run out of more advanced material to explore, having just gone as far as he could go in Maths within the school system; he had essentially academically outgrown High School and Sixth Form College provision for Maths at the grand old age of 12!

With A-Levels out the way the options for where to go next were fewer and the implications of decisions at this point potentially more damaging. It had been suggested that perhaps Cameron could now work on developing his Maths abilities in a sideways direction, undertaking further A-Level Maths modules that he had previously rejected when making his choices. After careful consideration it was felt that there were three major problems with this strategy; firstly Cameron had rejected these particular units for a reason, namely they weren't interesting or his "thing", secondly he was in this position because the A-Level material offered little challenge so why would more of the same help his intellectual development and keep him interested and thirdly because Cameron, like most children, has a burning need to see a tangible sign of success, whether it is an exam result or a chess trophy, and the sense of achievement and praise that it brings. In fact when it was mentioned to him, Cameron couldn't grasp why anyone would think he would want to do that, to him it seemed pointless! There were suggestions of Maths competitions as a possible direction but unfortunately this made Cameron extremely upset because, for him, Maths is the thing he loves and it would somewhat taint it for him if it was turned into some sort of competitive sport.

It is at this point that some would argue that this would be the stage to be considering university entry and in some cases have done so, but there was never any question of this being ever close to appropriate. We had refused to let Cameron be sent by the education authority to Sixth Form College because we felt it would have damaged his social and emotional development; an adult environment would have been worse. We could not see any way that a frankly socially immature boy (even for 12) would fit into an environment of young adults. On top of this is still the issue of the rest of his education to consider, since we were determined to ensure that Cameron gained a well rounded academic profile alongside his peers through the standard curriculum. Just how unsuitable it would have been for him to mix with older students was emphasised when he went to pick up his A-Level exam results. It was evident that he mixed awkwardly with the older pupils (being too shy to even ask what room he should be going to) and whilst the older pupils weren't unkind, we felt that he was a novelty or a curiosity. You may recall what we said before of Cameron's choice of "treat" for doing well in the exam; a visit to Toys'R'Us for some Doctor Who toy figures!

Given the success of distance learning with A-Level material, this was top of the list for future academic studies. To our mind there is really only one educational establishment with an established reputation in the UK for distance learning at tertiary level and that is the Open University (OU). With the Open University the student is able to choose from a wide range of courses at different levels and of different study durations. This allows the studying experience to be adapted to the individual student and their academic needs, interests and the time they have available to dedicate to study. Although the OU, in common with any other tertiary education establishment, is an adult only environment they do have a department that specifically deals with students who are under the age of 18. The Open University is actively working with many schools in the UK with their Young Applicants in Schools Scheme (YASS) which gives select post-16 year old students the opportunity to be able to study at a higher level, fitting around school work and social lives, encourages independent learning and building confidence and giving them a taste of university life from an academic perspective. Refreshingly, when considering any young applicant, they are very much mindful to make sure that it is the young person themselves wanting to pursue this study and further, whilst the young person may understand the subject matter, that they have the necessary skills to be able to communicate that understanding in an effective way. The OU even insists on checking with the young person's current school to ensure they don't believe it will interfere with their school studies. The support given by the OU not just in terms of academic support but additionally in pastoral support has been excellent.

Following initial discussions with the OU, and after Cameron was personally spoken to at Regional Director level, Cameron was able to start the level 1 course "The History of Maths" (TM190) (level 1 being the equivalent to the first year at a conventional university). Not only would this course be an introduction to study at a tertiary level of education but it offered Cameron the opportunity to be able to explore the backgrounds of material he had previously learnt and with a minimal commitment in terms of time (the course was a "10 point" course – full time university study in a year is 120 points). This allowed him to advance his studies and keep him stimulated at the same time as not overwhelming him while he was busy preparing for his exams.

This course would mean Cameron would be able to explore the contributions of different cultures to current mathematical thinking and would be able to look in more detail at discoveries that we currently take for granted, which was perfect for a child who continually wanted to know "why" and the background to everything he did. It was also an easy way to test how Cameron would cope not just with the academic material but also with the somewhat different approach of university study. By this stage of education a student is expected to do homework assignments, source additional resources and information and to meet deadlines without being reminded to do so by their teacher in the way that they are in high school. These are skills that are developed gradually as part of the process of becoming a young adult who is becoming more responsible for himself. On one occasion we asked a teacher why they hadn't helped Cameron with a question he had about presentation of his A-Level work. They stated that they had told him when they were free, where they would be and stated that he could come then if he wanted. This of course is perfectly sufficient to make a 17 or 18 year old who is motivated show up! We had to remind them that Cameron was 12 and that at that age they are generally simply told when and where to show up and that while he was indeed academically at A-Level he was still in most respects very much a 12 year old boy. Cameron also had to learn to express himself on paper, as verbally he could tell us all about what the various scholars achieved and how Maths developed for literally hours but when faced with an essay assignment would look at a blank screen and state he didn't know what to say!

It needs to be clearly noted that the move to degree level studies was done on the basis that it was the next logical step to take having proven himself at GCSE and A-Level, and was a decision that was not taken lightly. His entry was carefully managed at a minimum level of study and a great deal of effort was made ensuring that this was something that was seen as a source of enjoyment and not undue pressure, which was continually reviewed. About a year ago we were approached by a parent who felt that her 11 year old daughter was a gifted poet and songwriter but that her school were of no support whatsoever. Whilst some sympathy could be given if this were indeed the case, and it certainly wouldn't have been unheard of, the parent felt that her daughter should start studies with the Open University as a way of proving to her teachers that they were wrong. Our advice was asked in this matter as she saw Cameron as an example that it could be successfully done, ignoring the steps that he took in between. At no point was getting Cameron involved with the Open University a decision that was taken lightly. There is no question that actions such as suddenly throwing an 11 year old child straight into tertiary education can be misguided, dangerous to long term development and is the kind of behaviour that can contribute to giving parents of gifted children a bad name! Firstly, to start pursuing studies at degree level in this instance was not a logical step; her daughter had not even looked at GCSE or A-Level material and her sole basis for deciding her child was a prodigy was in reading short stories and songs her daughter had written. Secondly her motivation was in part driven by a desire to prove something and clearly was not purely based on what was in the best interests of her daughter. Advanced education is not a magic wand that will suddenly resolve any issues there may be of a school not meeting your child's needs, indeed if not done correctly it will just make the general situation worse. At each and every stage of the process with Cameron we have constantly kept enquiring what alternative options were available to our current course of action, checked that what Cameron is doing currently is still working for him and have been willing to totally change what we were doing if it didn't work, and indeed we frequently have. In other words all our actions have been completely centred on what best suited Cameron, not what was convenient for us or anyone else.

From that initial 10 point module with the Open University, Cameron went on to take a number of courses not just in Mathematics but also in Astronomy, which he was very interested in. At the age of 13 he successfully completed the Certificate in Mathematics (with distinction). He is currently enrolled in the Diploma of Mathematics programme which he is due to complete this year, and by the age of 16 he hopes to have completed the full Bachelor of Science Honours Degree. Achievements aside, every course which Cameron examines as a possibility is looked at by us, in conjunction with the Open University, as to whether or not he would be able to cope with the level of material and the workload involved. One course was rejected on the basis that while it was an excellent early course for most students, based as it was on everyday situations such as balancing a cheque book, it was precisely this reliance on knowledge of the adult world that made it totally unsuitable. Just because Cameron has great mathematical ability, doesn't mean that he is suited for all courses, making the Open University with their variety of options perfect for him. Great care was, and still is, taken in ensuring that the interest and hobby he has doesn't become a chore or a source of anxiety. At no point have these studies caused any disruption to his social or emotional development and if anything have helped it by allowing him to gain more of a sense of who he is and what he is capable of doing, making him more comfortable in his personal identity.

The great age competition is something which needs to be avoided and not drawn in to. The media are quick to point out the record for the youngest ever child to achieve such and such. This runs the risk of making parents and children believe that this is an essential element to their learning; to show how well they are doing by getting to set points at a younger age than anyone else. There was an article featured on the BBC website recently about a 5 year old girl who took a GCSE Maths exam and was awarded a Grade of E. This is, depending on the exam board and the year the exam was sat, most probably a mark of around 35%. To a certain extent it is true that doing this exam was an achievement for a child that young but what has this record actually proved? In our view it certainly proved that she wasn't intellectually ready to take the exam or she would have got an A or A*, as at GCSE and A-Level much of the material is based on rote learning of concepts and is fairly straight forward. Her father firmly maintained that he hadn't pushed his child into taking the exam, which raises several questions, not least of which is to wonder how many 5 year olds even know what a GCSE is! He went on to say, "I wouldn't say Maths is her favourite subject, but when she says she wants to be a doctor I tell her that she must be very good at science and Maths. We want her to be outstanding and exceptional in every way." This means that even by her father's own admission she isn't pursuing something she is particularly good at or even very interested in. Instead it is his freely admitted aim to make her "outstanding and exceptional", not happy or doing her best, and he is already starting her on an educational fast track to chase the notions of a 5 year old girl! Such actions lead one to ask just what exactly the education professionals involved with this child were doing, as Cameron wasn't allowed by his school to even contemplate taking his GCSE exam until he had undertaken a mock exam to see how he coped, not just with the material, but with the pressure of an exam situation. We have never pushed Cameron into any studies based on a determination to get there first, after all what advantage does this give a child long term? This attitude has become obsessive to the point where parents are boasting about their 7 month old children being gifted as they already know the alphabet; how can you tell and why precisely did it occur to you to try to teach it to them because it is somewhat doubtful that they asked you to!

Those in the media who promote these very early successes aren't so quick when it comes to looking at how the children concerned ultimately fair in later life. After all childhood is supposed to be a time of transition, of gradually maturing into a well-balanced adult, ready to cope with life and the world at large. If being the first past the post doesn't help achieve this, and indeed is detrimental to the child, then what exactly is the point of it? It's one thing to have a goal; its quite another when a parent hijacks that goal (or even forces that goal on a child) in pursuit of a meaningless record. After all, is being a parent not supposed to be all about doing your best for your child, not for yourself?

The Advisory Committee on Mathematics Education in the UK produced an extremely interesting report which looked at students who undertook

GCSE Maths exams early, which it comments has doubled in the past two years (2009 to 2011). In this report they place the reasoning for this on a "target driven culture". Many people understand the term "pushy parent" however the committee is keen to point out that there are also "pushy headteachers"; headteachers who want to see their school improve their ratings in league tables (grade C or higher in Maths is part of the official measure used by the Government). They went on to say "If any students are to be entered early, they must be confidently predicted to achieve an A*". Of concern is the observation that 25% of schools who choose to submit students early for GCSE Maths see these students then stop studying the subject once they achieve a Grade C, having achieved the necessary result for the school to be viewed as successful. The report further acknowledges that whilst early entry can be successful for a small number of high-achieving individuals, there should also be a suitable programme of further study to then progress the examinees towards A-level. It should be pointed out that in the vast majority of cases early entry is not in the child's best interests. The chairperson of the committee, Professor Dame Julia Higgins is quoted as saying "We are seeing a worrying increase in the numbers of students being entered early for GCSE mathematics, to the detriment of almost all students....It's no longer a case of a careful selection of the brightest students being pushed through early - it's whole cohorts now, whether or not it's in their long term interests as individuals." The committee has called on the government to see league tables revised in order to eliminate what it sees as incentives for schools to submit students early.

The Department for Education responded to the report stating "It's right that schools are free to make judgements about when their pupils are ready to take GCSEs. Ministers expect these decisions to be taken in pupils' best interests - so that the brightest are stretched and fulfil their potential and those that need support can achieve a good standard in Maths. We will reform league tables to get rid of any perverse incentives."

6   What's Wrong With Pushy?

Quite often we hear the term "pushy parent" used to denote a parent who works with their child to advance them beyond their peers, often in one specific area. In some cases this can be without an aptitude for the field in the mistaken belief that parents can force success on their child.

Lets get something straight; there is nothing essentially wrong with being a "pushy parent"; helping a gifted child achieve that little bit extra. Being "pushy" or perceived to be "pushy" is simply looking out for them as individuals; in helping them access opportunities and fulfilling their own potential. The fact of the matter is that even the best school is about the group; the class, the year group, the form, the set whereas parents are focused on the child as an individual. Of course with a school this is by necessity; after all even when a teacher does their best to consider each child separately, they simply can't afford to spend more time or give more attention to any one child to the detriment of the rest of the class. Teachers have the welfare of all their children to consider. It is all too easy to criticise schools and individual staff but despite our fair share of problems with various schools we can accept that often the staff are either in a difficult position or feel powerless to act within the guidelines of the education system. Understanding of giftedness and Asperger's Syndrome seems to have changed from year to year and often the views of the teacher are simply indicative of the year they qualified as teachers!

A school can no doubt tell you the breakdown of grades within a group; they will tell you what percentage of their school achieved an A*-C grade in a particular exam for a given year; a parent will tell you what his or her own child achieved, what subjects they are strong in and where they have difficulties as well as what comes easily to them and what areas are a fight every step of the way. If a child is finding school-work difficult it is perfectly reasonable for a parent to discuss extra work and support for their child. After all, there is an entire curriculum to be covered in school with the whole class while a parent can help their child at home to spend some extra time where it is needed. Anyway shouldn't a parent be able to spend time with their child at home helping them improve? Parents already listen to their younger children reading and most of us had homework every night when we were in primary school; nobody thought anything of it! Isn't better for children to do additional work at home that means they are kept stimulated, involved with learning and not disrupting the rest of the class' learning experience? Why too if a child is finding school-work easy shouldn't a parent go and see what can be done without being branded "pushy"?

Of course when we say there is nothing wrong with "pushy", that is not to say that it is acceptable to put undue pressure on children, force unreasonable demands and targets on them and to micro-manage every aspect of their lives, denying them the opportunity to learn life skills through their own experiences and indeed mistakes. Firstly childhood is not a competitive event, it is about your child doing their best, not someone else's best. Secondly nobody learns self-discipline when someone else takes away all the opportunities to develop it. Sometimes it is just necessary to let children stand on their own two feet on non-Earth shattering issues, let them fail and then suffer the consequences, gaining essential life experience. There are situations where parents can choose to use authority or they can choose to use influence; authority tells them what to do, influence helps them to reach the decision on their own. Of course there are times when for their own well-being we have to use authority but whenever possible involving a child in the decision develops important skills for later life. Dealing with failures themselves teaches children how to recover from them and how to deal with challenges in general. Of course a child should be sheltered to a certain degree from some of the harsh realities of life but this should certainly not be to the extent that they grow up with an unrealistic view of life and unprepared for what life may have in store. When a child is micro-managed then whenever they finally move out of their own sheltered bubble, they simply won't have the same amount of self-discipline skills already in place as someone who had been trusted at an earlier age. The diarist Anne Frank wrote this of children; "parents can only give good advice or put them on the right paths, but the final forming of a person's character lies in their own hands".

Perhaps one of the worst examples of poor parenting (conscious or not) is where children are seen by their parents as a second chance or a way to correct the missed opportunities of their own childhood. It is their child's life and they are individuals, not carbon copies of their parents or clay to be moulded into whatever shape their parents want them to be. The Daily Mail featured a fascinating interview with one such "pushy mother" whose daughter had taken their GCSE exams and was awaiting the results. The mother wrote "...I am guilty of putting my daughters under phenomenal pressure to succeed at school and perform well in exams. I'm terrified that if they aren't high achievers they won't survive in the cut-throat world of work they will enter once they leave education behind. In a nutshell, my husband and I did well for ourselves — so now, like most parents, we want our three girls, aged 16, 13 and five, to do even better...It's a part I've been playing since each of my youngsters was in nappies; ever since a news report claimed that reading to a baby was a brilliant way of firing up dormant brain cells. From that day on, even though my baby was just a couple of months old, I read to her every bedtime. And I did the same with her sisters when they came along.

Then, when a midwife friend told me that long-term breast-feeding was thought to boost intelligence, I seized that piece of much-debated information and ran with it. How could I not feed them until they were at least a year old after hearing that?

Meanwhile, I pushed them around in buggies that faced me, rather than the traffic, so I could talk to them on the way to the shops.

And I fed them brain-food, such as salmon and mackerel, and spent hours playing memory games and doing jigsaws on the floor.

Then, when they started school I made sure each of my children already knew their alphabet and could count to 20, ready for their teacher assessments in the first term...That way, they would start school life where I intended them always to stay — at the top of the class. Since then, I've been 'one of those mothers' — the kind who has the direct line to their child's head of year on speed-dial and repeatedly emails for updates on how they're getting on....And it's dawning on me, rather uncomfortably, she's fretting not so much because of the way she's handled these [GCSE] exams, but because of how I have.

In the run-up to them, 'no' was my default answer when she wanted to go out with her friends, stay up late or take a day off from her studies. 'This is your future,' I told her, almost daily. 'You can't take your eye off the ball, not for a moment.'

Now, I can't help but wonder whether, instead of encouraging her to succeed — which was what I intended — I've ended up having her believe she's simply not allowed to fail...It makes me wonder whether the grades our children are given will mean more to us than them. Having finally recognised the stress I've put my daughter under in recent months, that's something I feel bad about."

Those familiar with the programme Strictly Come Dancing may remember the judge and choreographer Arlene Philips. At the age of 68 and having already raised her daughter, Arlene went on record to say that she now feels her instincts as a "pushy parent" were misguided. Her daughter, Alana, now 31 was interviewed by the Daily Mail regarding her childhood experiences and this was what she had to say:

"Thinking back to my early childhood memories one image sticks out: it's me, walking to school with an enormous bag of books stuck on my back, like a turtle.

I was so tiny, perhaps six, and the books weighed almost as much as me. And if I wasn't waddling to school under the weight of my homework I was shuttling between all my extra-curricular activities.

Every hour of the day was filled from the moment I got up to the moment I went to bed. My ballet timetable alone was exhausting: I did an hour and a half on Mondays, half an hour on Tuesday, then two hours on Friday and Saturday.

It was just too much for a six-year-old, although I didn't know it at the time because I didn't know any different.

School itself was ultra-competitive, the kind of place where they had rehearsals for sports day — and there was piles of pressure. Luckily, I was pretty adaptable and very conscious of not wanting to let Mum down, so I just got on with it.

I had some amazing experiences, too, thanks to Mum's career. Not many children get to hang out in the south of France with Elton John, or on the set of countless pop videos. Even then, though, I always had a bag of books with me.

The funny thing is that I only knew how I really felt once my situation changed. Angus [stepfather] mellowed Mum. Under his influence I was allowed to be more of a tomboy, to climb trees and get muddy. I loved that, because in the past it wasn't unknown for Mum to get het up because I'd got a T-shirt dirty....

I was 11 when my sister was born, and she had a completely different experience to me — from the vantage point of being a young teenager it seemed that she could do whatever she wanted and I did resent it a bit. There seemed to be a lot of 'don't worry if you don't like it' and 'is that ok with you Abi?'

Maybe deep down that had some impact because as I got older I rebelled – drinking, staying out and not coming home. I put Mum and Dad through hell. Probably, though, it was just stupid teenage selfishness. Either way I now regret it bitterly.... She [Mum] now says: 'I can't believe I was so hard on you' and we laugh about it. I can't wait to have kids of my own and make her a grandmother. Of course, I like to think I'll be a relaxed parent, but I'll probably drive my children crazy while she's a chilled out grandma.

What I do know is that having drive is good, but not if it comes at the expense of your child's well-being".

All parents need to be able to accept the child that they have and help them do their best, not try to make them into someone else. The author Laurens Van Der Post said "The educating of the parents is really the education of the child; children tend to live what is unlived in the parents, so it is vital that parents should be aware of their inferior, their dark side, and should press on getting to know themselves". If it isn't what the child fundamentally wants, or if it makes them unhappy, then sooner or later they will end up resenting the situation, and in extreme cases the person who pushed them into that situation in the first place. Of course that is not to say that children should be allowed to jump from activity to activity without understanding the value of commitment and without giving something a fair try. What we are saying is that it simply isn't acceptable to force children long term into activities that they don't want to do and there is a world of difference between motivated parenting and obsessive parenting. But what is really wrong with wanting, arguing and fighting for what is best for your children and doing what you can to ensure they develop into well rounded balanced individuals? The fact is that it's the children of interested parents who are most likely to succeed.

Too many parents are being branded "pushy parents" when they challenge those within education, which is ironic considering the amount of time schools spend trying to encourage parental involvement and trying to eliminate apathy. Actively pursuing opportunities for our child that can maximise future success is one of the greatest gifts we can give. It is the "pushy parents" that can improve the outlook for all children not just their own, for example in holding schools to account over standards. Such actions up the game for all pupils; if there is a failure to provide for one child then they will likely be a similar failure for another. In the past when we asked primary teachers for increased input for Cameron it was treated as an inconvenience and sometimes even as a threat. For all that Parent/Teacher conferences always preached about the importance of parental involvement, the minute we stated our belief that Cameron would benefit from studying at a higher level, we were suddenly being unreasonable and everything they were doing was sufficient. We can only hope that the results of the later tests at high school and the level that Cameron's Maths settled at naturally will have ultimately altered how they deal with the situation if they come across it again, that they might watch for the signs of a gifted child from now on. A profoundly gifted child may be the only one present in that school at that time but if new systems are put in place to recognise and provide for gifted children then, sooner or later, others will benefit. Teachers may understand education but ultimately it is the parent that understands their own child.

Whether or not you would define someone as a "pushy parent" in the traditional, negative way comes down to several key questions:

- Are the parents pushing for something the child wants to do?

- Is the child capable of the level or ability which the parents are pushing   for?

- Is there a balance within the child's life between social, emotional and intellectual needs or is there a single-minded focus on one specific aspect?

- Are the parents prepared to take on board valid constructive advice or are they only interested in hearing positive feedback in relation to their child?

- Are the parents hijacking a child's hobby or interest and turning in into something they no longer enjoy?

Whether or not you consider someone a "good pushy parent" or a "bad pushy parent" comes down to balance and motivation. The "bad pushy parent" is often seen to have a fixation on one aspect of their child's development. At its extreme this becomes "hothousing" (which can never be good) where the parent blindly pushes their child down a particular path usually, if not always, to the detriment of other aspects of development. The focus solely becomes intellectual development, and indeed a subset at that, and nothing else matters. These children spend hours on end studying to the exclusion of any other interests or even just playing, on their own or with friends. These may seem simplistic activities but they play a vital part in social and emotional development. We have seen parents of young children in documentaries where they state that their children do other activities, then give a number of hours spent studying each day so large that it completely precludes them doing anything else! Advocates of hothousing argue that it is an essential tool for the gifted to be able to flourish intellectually; periods of intense study of a topic are necessary in order to stimulate their child's mind. This means that as children their intellectual development is curtailed to within a narrow focus and their chances of social and emotional development are lessened.

These are the children that are packed off to university at a young age. Despite the talent that Cameron has shown for Maths, would it be right for us as parents to choose a career path for him at a very early stage? For those parents whose children who are sent off to university at a young age, and where their education moves from the broad skill set of secondary school to the narrow field constituting a degree, are making a big assumption and a decision as to their child's future direction that is more than premature. Cameron may be well a gifted mathematician but he should still have the same options open to him at the age of 17/18 as his peers, even though he will have a few extra achievements under his belt. Traditional universities that accept children into their ranks really need to question why they choose to let this happen (the Open University is not included in this statement for reasons given in Chapter 4) as they, more than most, should recognise that the children, and this term is used advisedly here, that join their faculties early aren't ready to join the adult world of tertiary education. There appears to be little regard for the social and emotional development of the child in these actions. It is in knowing that some universities choose to accept children that validate the actions of the hothousing parent, whether intentional or not, and allows them to set goals of seeing their children in University at a young age.

Consider the case of Sufiah Yusof who first made headlines in 1997 when she gained entry into St Hilda's College, Oxford to study mathematics at the age of 13. In 2001, she ran away from her student flat in Oxford, after taking her final examination paper for the academic year. She was found working as a waitress in a Bournemouth Internet café two weeks later, but refused to return home, alleging that her parents made life difficult for her. She described her father as both bullying and controlling; no doubt her father felt that what he was doing was giving her the best start in life. In March 2008, it was discovered that after many ups and downs in her life she had finally experienced a "living descent to hell" in her life, to the point that she felt she had to prostitute herself to survive. She had come to the point where she believed her life had been completely destroyed and it took her many years to recover. One of her friends described her change of fortunes as "desperately heartbreaking", adding that "her gift [for Mathematics] really has been a curse". It should be noted that Sufiah ultimately did not pursue a career in Mathematics and is now working as a Social Worker; it must be said again that just because a child has a gifting in a specific field does not give the parents the right to select that for them as a career choice. Sufiah has deliberately chosen to abandon Mathematics so what presumably brought her happiness initially had become tainted. It could also be seen as significant that she chose Social Services as an alternative career, to try and help others.

There are countless other examples. One of these is the noted philosopher John Stuart Mill who found that the intensive study had a significant effect on his mental health and state of mind. His father had deliberately set out to develop a genius intellect in his son, restricted his interactions with other children to his siblings and home schooled him, beginning by teaching him Greek at 3. At the age of 20 he suffered a nervous breakdown. In chapter 5 of his Autobiography, he stated that this was caused by the "great physical and mental arduousness" of his studies which had suppressed any feelings he might have developed normally in childhood. This is a clear example of a hothoused child coming forward as an adult to state that their social and emotional development had been severely damaged. This case clearly demonstrates the fact that the risks associated with pushing a child into advanced education at an early age and seriously damaging their development has been known for some time, as John Stuart Mills was born in 1806!

Having considered the issues in terms of the gifted child, it is worth looking at the flip-side of the coin; is it really doing anyone any favours by encouraging a child to pursue an interest which they show no aptitude or talent for? Consider the auditions for programmes such as X-Factor and Britain's Got Talent where individuals leave in tears having been told they will never make it in the world of entertainment and having become the object of public ridicule and derision. In many cases these were people that were told by their well-meaning friends and family that they were brilliant, destined for a life of stardom, and the reality of being told the opposite is a crushing blow. It would seem that at no point did their family ever think to say that maybe singing or performing wasn't where their talents lay, leaving it instead to several celebrity judges and the laughter of the viewing public to let them know the truth. Many are further taken in by the advice of dubious "singing coaches" over that of their family and friends. Apparently that someone may have greater regard for their tuition fee than whether or not their pupil can actually sing never occurs to many people; they believe a professional singing coach will always tell you the truth! Of course that it not to slur those who work in this field but merely to point out that in every profession there are those who are more motivated by personal financial gain than by the best interests of their clients. Many people come to believe that constant practice has overcome the simple fact that they are tone deaf! What might these people have done with their lives if they hadn't wasted all their time on a fruitless pursuit? By all means sing because you enjoy it but know your strengths and weaknesses. These issues sadly don't just apply to the area of singing. We live in a society where children are being told that they can be whatever they want to be – obviously aptitude and talent no longer apply!

Those who are gifted tend to have a natural inclination towards a specific area or areas. What then happens to them to develop their talent, or not, is nurture. The big debate of nature verses nurture is one which is centuries old and no doubt will continue long into the future. Where there is ability without it being nurtured, the child is unlikely to flourish; they need stimulation and guidance and, depending on their particular type of gift, training or education to help them develop their potential. On the other hand nurture without a natural gift or ability with which to start is more likely to ultimately cause misery, as the child struggles to become something that they aren't. While they fight through an area that doesn't suit them, they neglect areas of endeavour that would suit their natural ability better. Blindly encouraging a child down a path with a mistaken belief that they have a gift is not good parenting. By encouraging them down the wrong path one denies the opportunity to them of exploring other avenues where a genuine aptitude exists. Why tell someone they can make it as a professional entertainer selling millions of albums around the world when their true skill may be, for example, as a Scientist? Ultimately they are highly unlikely to succeed in life as a balanced and happy individual. Their social and emotional development becomes damaged, especially if they are following the unsuitable path to please someone else.

Unfortunately to many people a child who shows an aptitude within an academic subject must be deemed to be the product of "pushy parents". After all, children can only be interested in football, popular music and computer games, or so we would be led to believe. Why is it that society has such a problem with academic talents?

It is regrettable that the fear of being labelled a "pushy parent" and being associated with the negative connotations of this term that many parents feel that there is little or no practical value to be gained in investigating whether or not their child may be "gifted and talented". These parents are scared of the way other parents, their families, their children's teachers or society may view and treat them. However it is worth remembering that it is knowledge of the pattern of cognitive strengths and weaknesses of their child that can help parents to plan the best learning experiences and ultimately give their children the best start in life.

7 Giftedness & Special Needs

Autistic Spectrum Disorders

It became obvious from a very early stage that with Cameron there was more than just him simply being clever. The words "eccentric" and "odd" had occurred on a fairly regular basis throughout his childhood (albeit in a nice way), with a certain amount of fond amusement generated in adult friends of the family when it came to describing the way he expressed himself. He was displaying a large vocabulary and an unusual way of expressing himself that was already noticeable from his first year in primary school. Unbeknownst to us at this point one of the characteristics of Asperger's Syndrome is an over-precise use of language.

At the very beginning of his school career Cameron's desperation to develop academically was already highly visible to us as his parents. We had hoped that his constant need to know more and more would find some satisfaction and outlet in school but unfortunately due to where his birthday falls Cameron was initially only allowed to attend half days at school until after the Christmas holidays. We unsuccessfully argued against this policy after only a few weeks because frankly we felt that far from having a "separation anxiety" from his parents, he was more upset by having to be removed from school at lunchtime each day; he use to cry all the way home because he wasn't allowed to stay for the remainder of the day. It was at this point where the first significant sign became apparent of his aptitude for Mathematics; having been casually told over cooking the dinner that 0 wasn't the lowest number, and having demanded to be told all about negative numbers, he promptly went to school the next day and corrected his teacher on her "error" of the previous day. With hindsight, there should probably have been massive warning bells ringing at this stage! As time passed Cameron's academic ability became more marked.

On another front, for us as his parents anyway, it was becoming more and more obvious that socially Cameron was out of step with his peers despite his desperation to fit in. He was a friendly and sociable boy, and indeed has now become a friendly young man (despite describing himself on TV as having the "social ability of a talking potato"), who has been described as "charming" with his open and honest manner and sharp, slightly self-deprecating sense of humour. It was never the case that he didn't want to socially fit in, it was just that he actually, for all his intelligence, wasn't capable of it.

For many years everyone around him was quite convinced he had Asperger's Syndrome. Cameron's sister Emma had long since been diagnosed as being autistic, so we had a certain understanding of Autistic Spectrum Disorders. We had become gradually convinced in the latter years of Cameron's primary school years as he failed to mature in his understanding of others in ways that his sister Beth, 3 and a half years his junior, was grasping instinctively. If they went to a playground they would always find other children to play with, but it was Beth who would find them and start the games off. Cameron had the will, but lacked the ability to do it. It was becoming increasingly obvious that Cameron generally got on best with children younger than him in a non-academic setting, in other words less mature and slightly less socially developed than his peers, something which persists to this day. We knew several people with Asperger's Syndrome who had some similarities to Cameron in their difficulties, although to different degrees and this, in conjunction with what we researched ourselves when we investigated, left us convinced he had the condition. As time, and his first couple of years of high school passed, the concept of Cameron having Asperger's became gradually more accepted by most of the teaching professionals surrounding him, although this was sometime before his formal diagnosis. In fact when we recently contacted the high school he spent his first year in to let them know how he was doing we mentioned that he had been diagnosed with Asperger's. Suffice to say that this was met with a decided lack of surprise!

Having such a "condition" as Asperger's Syndrome puts Cameron in distinguished company alongside Bill Gates, Albert Einstein, Sir Isaac Newton, Mozart, Michelangelo and Thomas Edison, although it is also notable that several of these people are well known in history for a certain degree of eccentricity sitting alongside their genius! This is not to say that all gifted children have Asperger's (nor that all children with Asperger's are gifted) but it is certainly of note the number who do towards the top end of gifted spectrum where the child is significantly ahead of their peers in areas such as Maths, science or engineering.

It is worth noting that those with Asperger's Syndrome, while being at the top end of the Autistic Spectrum, have in common with the rest of it a tendency towards using systems to understand the world around them. A basic explanation of this would be trying to apply if $x + y = z$ to everything in life, including the rather more flexible arenas such as interacting socially with others. To quote Professor Simon Baron-Cohen, one of the worlds foremost experts on Autism, discussing Asperger's Syndrome, "People with the condition...share the social and communication difficulties of those with classic autism, as well as the narrow - even obsessive - interests and love of repetition." It is in working within an academic area they can be extremely well suited! He has also discussed how "good attention to detail and a good understanding of systems" is valuable in mathematics, why Maths suits many with Asperger's Syndrome and how a pre-natal test for Autistic Spectrum Disorder could have serious repercussions for the future. He asks, "Would we also reduce the number of future great mathematicians, for example?".

As we have said, just because someone is highly intelligent or gifted in one particular way and is somewhat quirky doesn't mean they have Asperger's. Nor does someone who interacts poorly with others automatically have to be "Autistic". There is a fashion recently to describe those who are perceived to have problems on some occasions working with others as being, "a bit autistic", as if it had suddenly become an adjective. During his time as Prime Minister this was a term that increasingly was applied to Gordon Brown, with the context it was used in some cases making it virtually an insult. This is the doubled-edged sword of the Autistic Spectrum, in all its various degrees, becoming more widely recognised and in the public eye. With greater visibility comes the risk of greater misunderstanding, especially when the term Autistic Spectrum covers such a vast area; from children who are completely shut off from the world around them to those who are highly intelligent, but socially slightly off kilter. During the 1980's and early 1990's many people associated the term "autistic" with the movie "Rain Man" in which Dustin Hoffman played the part of a young man with an astounding recall for baseball facts; in fact the character he played suffered from Savant Syndrome which is only associated with autism in 50% of cases. On a positive note at least the character was sympathetic and started people questioning what provisions there actually are for those on the autistic spectrum.

Asperger's Syndrome is something that most people can't tell about someone from looking at them; at worst perhaps most people may judge them as being different. Unlike conditions such as Down's Syndrome for example, there are no clear physical signs of Asperger's and the diagnostic process is complex and can take a considerable amount of time. This is more than partly because many children exhibit at least one of what may be considered to be the standard signs of Asperger's; it is all about the severity and the interaction of these different traits, as well as a certain view of the world. It is therefore important that this assessment is properly done to ensure children that are shy or maybe have behavioural issues don't get given the wrong label. Aside from any other considerations, such as possible social stigma, any incorrect diagnosis of a child can lead either to them missing out on available help or having systems put in place for them that are completely ineffective for the child in question because they are designed to work with something they haven't got!

We came to our conclusion about Cameron only after many years of research, years of being Cameron's parents watching the same patterns emerge again and again and finally speaking to those with personal experiences of Asperger's. On the other hand the sentence beginning the paragraph above states "most people" on purpose. For parents, teachers and those otherwise involved with those with Asperger's Syndrome there are occasions when on meeting someone for the first time they might as well have a neon sign over their head! This doesn't mean that it is up for discussion though as many parents are understandably concerned about their children being treated differently, in an adverse way, if their "condition" is widely known.

What is important to note is that irrespective of any diagnostic label that is attached to a child, every child is unique. There can be a reluctance amongst both parents and professionals to apply such an impersonal thing as a "label" to a child. For some time, mainly when we were busy trying to find out Cameron's Maths "level" and find out the best way to provide for his unusual needs, we didn't push too hard for formal diagnosis as we already knew in our own heads and didn't feel it made much difference to us as his parents. It can also, sadly, be very hard to get the ball rolling on an assessment for suspected Asperger's Syndrome. After all, for the education department the child isn't falling behind and assessments are expensive. Additionally (and this may merely be the view of two very jaded, and now somewhat cynical, parents who've had to fight long and hard for some things to be provided), educational departments don't have to pay for provisions if no one has been able/allowed to make a diagnosis!

A diagnosis of Asperger's doesn't define a child, it merely offers an insight into where their strengths and weaknesses may lie and provides direction in what support may be needed. Cameron was Cameron both before the diagnosis and after it. A label doesn't map out or control their lives but it opens doors for possible help. No two children with Asperger's are the same but then the same can be said about children in general. The advice for parents of children with Asperger's is no different to the advice given to any parent; provide a supportive and loving home environment, know your child's strengths and weaknesses and give them as much support, patience, and understanding as you can. A label of Asperger's (or any label for that matter) is simply a tool that can be used to get your child what support and services they may need to get their best chance in life; there is really no need to panic about having that label.

Professionals can be so concerned about the effect a diagnostic label can have on a child's parents that they will hold off even when they are certain, waiting until they feel the parents are ready to hear it. This happened with our middle child, Emma, and we didn't thank them for it! After all, if it hadn't been for that course of action Emma would have been receiving educational services over 6 months earlier than she did. When your child is 3 and still in nappies, unable to talk, only drinks from a baby's bottle and eats with her fingers, what parent wouldn't want any education services available asap! How much longer would it have been if we hadn't gone and confronted them, having realised that something was going on? No matter what label is applied to them, children are still the same people they always were. We have 3 children and, in age order, they are at this point in time 1) 14, in high school with Asperger's Syndrome and well through a Maths degree, 2) 12, in a Special Needs school, can't talk, still wears nappies, needs constant help with self-care and can't read or write but is still happy and fulfilled and 3) 10, in primary school and intelligent but "typically developing". However they are so much more than that, they are three children with all the positives and negatives that implies and, most importantly, they are Cameron, Emma and Bethany! Any labels they may have are part of them but by no means define them. Parents can be left with the impression of a label as the end of the world; it isn't at all and doesn't change a child but it may change the way they are interacted with for the better. We don't feel this can be emphasised strongly enough, so again; it is merely a tool to give all-important access to services that will help your child, it does not and will not diminish them in any way, unless it is allowed to, therefore don't!

What then exactly is Asperger's Syndrome? It is a form of Autism which affects how a person makes sense of the world and is significantly more prevalent in boys than in girls. This fact is something that is currently continually being researched, not least of all by Professor Simon Baron-Cohen at Cambridge University. Some have referred to Asperger's as a "swiss cheese" type of development: some things are learned age-appropriately, some may be learnt early (sometimes years ahead) whilst other things may lag behind or be absent. They have a strong aptitude for focussing on the minutia of a task and function best when working with a topic that has patterns and clear cut ways of behaving, that always follows a set of rules. This is why Maths and engineering are particularly suitable and naturally attractive for many of those with Asperger's Syndrome. Professor Baron-Cohen hypothesises that it is in no way a coincidence that the majority of those with Asperger's are male and that the majority of those studying Mathematics or engineering at university are also male.

This provides the reason why, in addition to the ethical and eugenics debate implications, Professor Baron-Cohen believes any future decision to offer a pre-birth test for autism, in the event such a thing is created, should be carefully examined concerning its implications on the intellectual capabilities of the population. This isn't to say that all those with Asperger's Syndrome are therefore going to want to be mathematicians or engineers. Nor that all mathematicians or engineers have Asperger's! Once again the situation, as with many things in life, is nowhere near that absolute and all children, whether they have a diagnostic label or not, should be treated as the individuals that they are.

Asperger's Syndrome is part of a broad diagnostic category referred to as "Autistic Spectrum Disorders". This is where all those who have Autism or who are described as Autistic fall. While all those on it share a number of traits in common, they otherwise differ vastly to the point where the spectrum is wide enough to include children who are totally closed off and spend much of their time rocking back and forth and are totally incapable of coping with any form of change to Cameron, in mainstream school but sailing through university level Maths. Those who have Asperger's are generally considered to have a higher intellectual capacity while at the same time have, often significant, problems in understanding social situations, non-verbal behaviours and seeing everything in a very literal way. Recently Cameron began expressing a strong interest in the opposite sex in the way teenage boys do, and a sarcastic comment was made suggesting that perhaps a cold shower might be appropriate; needless to say about 3 minutes later the sound of running water was heard....followed by a frantic parental dash for the bathroom!

Social situations don't have a set of hard and fast rules, what is appropriate in one situation isn't in another. Most of us have the ability to judge these things instinctively, and can tell when the mood in a room or situation has changed on a subconscious level. If someone insisted that we explain how exactly we knew, we would be hard pushed to give a precise reason, which is exactly what Cameron often wants and needs to be given. This then is the problem for Cameron and others like him with Asperger's Syndrome; that they can't spot these things themselves as they lack the capability. The rules of social interaction are unwritten and complex and those who understand are not able to give rigid rules that apply to every situation as they frankly don't exist! For example Cameron has got himself in trouble with his peers on numerous occasions down the years for apparently boasting about things ranging from the games consoles he owns to his abilities and achievements. The problem is that Cameron doesn't actually think that way. It doesn't occur to him that telling a child whose family can't afford these things would be insensitive and can be a fast way to lead to a confrontation, whether verbal or physical. From his point of view it was a fact that our family owned these things so what reason was there not to mention it? He was horrified when he was told that the effect he was having on others. Another example of brutal, factual honesty in action is from one of Cameron's friend who also has Asperger's. While we were out one day, getting over a bad case of the cold we met him and his family. The first thing he said when approaching us, even before saying hello, was announce that our noses' were incredibly red! We were obviously amused but had to explain carefully why that level of honesty about someone's appearance really wasn't a good idea!

Cameron has found himself several times in high school being drawn into physical confrontations when he has been discussing with his friends, in a casual manner, what he has been recently studying in Maths. Cameron's friends have come to accept his mathematical ability and achievements as simply who he is however whilst Cameron is happily talking to his friends about recent Maths successes, in the same way any teenager shares what is going on in their lives, those who aren't doing so well but are standing within earshot think he is having a go at them. Frankly this level of social complexity is beyond Cameron's grasp, the very idea just puzzles him! Therefore we, his teachers and several youth group leaders down the years have had to explain to Cameron not just that he can't do something but also attempt to explain why, in a way he can understand, otherwise he is doomed to repeat it. Hopefully he can create a mental rule for himself so that he won't make the same mistakes again and again. It is the explanation that is frequently most important for him, as Cameron has a desperate urge to understand everything. Of course none of this is to say that Cameron isn't competitive, just not when it comes to Maths. Console and computer games, where he and other children frequently compare scores, progress and tactics, are a totally different matter!

One of the other common features that can be often seen in those with Asperger's is an extreme almost if not actually obsessional interest in minute detail of what they are interested in, and conversely a complete disregard for anything which doesn't. There can be an extreme focus on particular subjects or interests to the point where they are practically encyclopedic on that topic but know virtually nothing about other subjects that they could reasonably be expected to know. Cameron can talk at length about the political machinations and factions behind the game play of the World of Warcraft computer game but doesn't know who the Deputy Prime Minister is. He can quote long and intricate plots from Doctor Who but had no idea who Lady GaGa was. When told of the death of Michael Jackson, Cameron wanted to know which football team he played for! It is common in cases of Asperger's that general knowledge is limited, due so much being outside their specific interests. Much of Cameron's general knowledge is gleaned from "The Simpsons", the satirical cartoons in "Private Eye" or from the "Horrible" books, lightweight in terms of effort it takes to absorb the content because he really dislikes reading. On the other hand he enthusiastically reads in depth Maths textbooks! The holes in Cameron's logic and knowledge can be completely unexpected, like discovering he planned to finish a postal assignment for the Open University the evening before the due date with no thought at all for how long the postal system might take but he knows what it means "to Vogue" because it was in "The Simpsons"!

One of the key problems we have found with Cameron is that he is "black and white" in his thinking. There is nothing in between; either something is or it isn't, which is characteristic of Asperger's. Whenever he undertakes something it is either a success or a failure; this has caused real problems for him when he receives academic results, especially in Maths. Combined with the fact that he spent so many years getting 100% because the work was far too easy means that he believes he is failing when he is getting marks of over 70%. This is a trend often associated with gifted children that if they are used to getting high marks they will come to see anything less than a grade A as a failure. Perfectionism is also a common trait with gifted children who come to associate their self-esteem with achieving high marks. These two factors can cause a gifted child to become utterly afraid of failure and avoid risking anything less than a perfect score, causing them to avoid the risk of new experiences. They may also become so sensitive to their own expectations, and those of others, that they feel enormous guilt over any marks they perceive as too low.

Cameron carries this success or failure attitude to all areas to his life and can be completely devastated when things don't quite work out which has lead to a few inedible breakfasts in bed still being eaten! He has experienced difficulties in understanding graduations in subjects such as politics as he tries to shed the simplistic view of everything either as good or evil, right or wrong. He is only now starting to really comprehend that there are grey areas in life, even though he still finds it very hard to spot them! He also has problems with contradictions, pragmatism and deception; his brain simply isn't wired that way! This returns us back to the fact that those with Asperger's Syndrome find it extremely difficult to grasp abstract concepts.

As with everything there are variations in what this limitation on creativity means for different people. Lacking imagination has never been an issue for Cameron, however greater than average creativity is part of being a gifted child. Cameron's imagination has always been restricted though to within the areas he is interested in. For example the summer he was 8 he was obsessed with Lord of the Rings while at a Kids Camp. Every time the boys in his group got bored they would turn to Cameron, who could be relied on to come up with an intricate Lord of the Rings-based war game for them all to play! Sometimes his random comments were a source of great amusement with the now infamous "look into my armpit and see the future". On the other hand he is still incapable of storywriting and even now has trouble writing essays about Maths down on paper.

We have found consistently that the best motivator for Cameron is a well defined goal. He is most comfortable when he knows clearly where he stands now, what he is aiming for and exactly what steps he has to do to get there. This is perhaps one of the biggest reasons why Cameron has progressed though the courses that he has; what is expected is clearly laid out that "if I learn x I will be able to achieve y". We have also found that when it comes to more artistic subjects and sporting endeavours the problem has been that there is a perceived lack of a clearly defined aim, or as Cameron put it "they aren't logical". When asked for a Educational Psychology test what his favourite subject was and why, Cameron stated Maths and that it was because it was logical, with Art as his least favourite because it wasn't logical. This is yet another illustration of this "black and white" thinking at work, as well as a failure to be able to understand something where success or failure is subjective. As there is no clear formula for success, Cameron dismisses it as being impossible to understand; understanding being a driving need for him. The lack of imagination that is often part of Asperger's doesn't effect Cameron's ability to play creative games but makes Art beyond him, as well as causing him great difficulty for parts of his Maths studies when he had to visualise 3D shapes.

Another aspect of the Asperger's Syndrome frequent lack of imagination can be in an inability to understand how and what others think. The putting aside of personal perspective, the ability to put themselves in someone else's shoes can be extremely difficult. This can cause difficulties with empathy and explaining concepts. It should be made clear here that empathy is the ability to understand the feelings of others. That is not the same as sympathy but is a problem that causes difficulties with understanding how a situation would affect someone else, which when combined with problems reading social cues and body language, means it can be hard for someone with Asperger's to figure out how someone feels. However when they realise, or someone tells them, how another person feels that does not mean that they will be lacking in sympathy. The problem with explaining a concept is that it requires understanding the point of view of someone who knows absolutely nothing about it. Once we were trying to check what mistake Cameron had made in an Open University question which used a specific kind of chart. Even as his parents, who are used to trying to get comprehensible answers out of him, it took five attempts to get an answer that made sense and assumed no prior knowledge!

There are disadvantages to having very narrow, and possibly incredibly in-depth interests, beyond just social or academic arenas. There are consequences for physical development and health. It was apparent from a very young age that Cameron did not have the interest or aptitude for sports and where possible he avoided sports, his preference was always to sit in front of a computer or to read computer games manuals. Apart from a general disinterest, Cameron didn't have any motivation to play team games such as football. While it is true that the point of football is clear enough for most people, namely to score more goals than the other team, we always found that Cameron struggled in seeing the point of it all. After all, as someone who is not naturally blessed with good co-ordination, the odds of Cameron actually scoring a goal, or even of being passed the ball, were never good so what immediate incentive did he have to play? Nobody enjoys humiliating themselves for little or no reward! Cameron's dislike of football had grown to the point that by the end of junior school he stated he had two sets of friends; those he played with generally and those he played with when his usual friends were playing football. As an avoidance tactic it certainly shows ingenuity, as well as his determination to not play football unless it was part of a PE class! This presented a problem, with obvious consequences for health.

Sufficient evidence exists to show the important health benefits of exercise in children (as we have referred to earlier), both now and in setting good habits for the future, but equally to force someone to do something they don't want to do is counter-productive and potentially damaging long-term. If a child is forced into a physical activity then they are unlikely to try their best and will probably quit at the first opportunity! After a certain element of trial and error, one activity surfaced as being highly successful and one which we have found a lot of parents of children with Autistic Spectrum Disorders choose. Martial Arts. Far from teaching children to be violent which some parents believe, Martial Arts has been the perfect activity for Cameron for a number of reasons:

- a good Martial Arts School is not just about the physical techniques but it's also about the attitudes and mental aspects that go hand in hand with the physical aspects; such as self-control, perseverance, self-discipline and focus. These are useful skills and attitudes for anybody, but for children anywhere on the

Autistic Spectrum or gifted children they are additionally important in the effect they will have on other areas of their life.

- clearly defined goals resulting in progression through the belt ranks until ultimately they reach the coveted "Black Belt". This fulfils the need of children with Asperger's to have systems as they know that if they learn certain techniques, or combinations of techniques, and katas well enough and behave in class then they will pass their Grading. It is a logical progression which is easy to understand and is coupled with clear and frequent rewards. Of course everyone likes success and to have their efforts rewarded!

- a high-energy, intense whole body exercise with plenty of variety which provides an outlet for energy, improves both physical condition and general health and keeps children's interest. An activity that improves fitness is specially useful for children who spend much of their time on one non-physical activity, whether that is their gift, their obsession or even both! Modern Martial Arts with its interactive nature, frequent changes of activity and fun games making learning fun are perfect for both those on the Autistic Spectrum and gifted children.

- Martial Arts develops self-discipline, focus and concentration which for gifted children only enhances their chances of making the most of their abilities. For children with Asperger's Syndrome it brings out the focus they often have naturally and helps develop it, teaching them to use it in different areas of their life. Plus it is beneficial for any child to work on skills that help them achieve whatever they can in school and life in general!

- self-confidence is improved by better fitness and also the knowledge that they have the capability to defend themselves means that they are confident in confrontational situations and are less likely to find themselves being bullied. This is examined in further detail below.

- the achievements and success of gifted children can cause jealousy and resentment, creating a risk of their being bullied.

- children with Asperger's Syndrome tend not to share the same interests as their peers, or at least not in the same spread, as they are more inclined to have a narrow focus. They also have difficulty understanding social rules such as turn-taking in conversations and that what is appropriate to say in one situation, isn't in another. There are also problems with reading body language, which can be what tells a person when they aren't welcome or when their audience is bored or irritated and they have difficulty understanding that in life honesty is not always the best policy. Just because something is true or factual doesn't mean that it being said out loud will be welcomed! This contributes to a greater likelihood of their being a target of bullying.

Good Martial Arts schools teach practical skills to both avoid and resolve confrontation, and not just in a physical way. They should teach confidence and how to stand tall and talk with self-assurance, which helps give the impression of confidence. Being self-confident in situations is like any skill in that it gets better with practice! Just knowing that he can defend himself if necessary gives Cameron confidence which projects through his voice and body language, frequently meaning that the physical aspect of a confrontation doesn't happen or is over quickly. There have been a number of occasions when someone attempted to strike Cameron, or one of his friends, and he has simply blocked the kick or punch so that it failed to make contact and that has ended the problem. The skinny, geeky little boy isn't supposed to suddenly produce a Martial Arts technique! The sheer uncertainty that creates of what else he might be capable of, surprise at the failure, coupled with the humiliation of failing to touch someone who was expected to be an easy target, means that the attacker often backs off. In addition news of an event like that spreads quickly. Cameron was once forced to defend himself and defeated a bully and, when he came home, stated that he didn't think it would make any difference as only five other people had seen it happen. With our rather better knowledge of how the world works we reassured Cameron that five witnesses was more than enough; we were proved right!

It was our personal experiences of the benefits of Martial Arts for both ourselves and our daughter and what it gave to Cameron and other children on the Autistic Spectrum or with ADHD that brought us to become interested in becoming Instructors. It taught both our children, but especially Cameron, how to deal with bullies without fighting but also self-defence if they couldn't avoid the bully or talk their way out of it. When Cameron moved onto high school it gave him more confidence to stand up for himself verbally, making it clear that he wasn't going to be an easy target. It vastly improved his co-ordination and balance and found him something physical that he was actually good at! Learning sequences of techniques (katas) was particularly satisfying for him because it gave him a chance to use his talent for memorisation.

Martial Arts also works in teaching children respect for themselves and others as well as the art of paying attention. Practising listening to someone, focussing just on them even for a short period is invaluable for children with any kind of special needs. While teaching Martial Arts we have worked with many children on improving their ability to perform basic social skills such as talking clearly while facing someone and mostly looking them in the eye! Just achieving that can make a vast difference to a child's life.

If we consider a child like Cameron with Asperger's who is working at degree level but has problems socially, then it is obvious that a lot of attention needs to be given to teaching social skills and advancing social development. Gifted children need to spend time on developing other areas in their life especially the social and emotional development which is a crucial component of growing up, and working towards becoming a well-rounded person. A child with Asperger's Syndrome has problems socially because much of social interaction is non-verbal. Sending a gifted child with Asperger's, two states which individually cause issues socially, to university to satisfy an intellectual need becomes even more questionable when the real area that needs additional attention is social and emotional development. At university they will indeed be removed from the presence of their peers who they can have difficulty interacting with due to areas where they differ from them but they won't have an easier time socially at university. Certainly they are less likely to encounter confrontation on a face-to-face basis but that doesn't mean that they will be accepted or will blend into campus life. They will have little in common with the other students beyond their academic interests, won't be able to socialise in many of the same places and will have just lost many of their chances to be with those at roughly the same stage of social development as they are. A child with Asperger's Syndrome would find university even more unsettling.

To refer to Asperger's as a "disability" or a "handicap" denies and belittles the fact that many people have been very successful in their careers, not despite their condition, but because of it. Using their abilities to understand systems and a capability to understand a subject they love in near obsessive detail is perfect for the fields of Maths and science. Children with Asperger's can and do learn to manage their differences successfully even though they may continue to find social situations and personal relationships challenging. Cameron has always maintained a small number of friends with the same interests as himself, who accept him for who is, although he did describe one particular group of them as all the "social misfits" sticking together! Those with Asperger's have to work harder at their social and emotional development because they don't develop the instinctive, unthinking knowledge of all the unsaid undercurrents of conversations or situations that most people have. The symptoms though can be camouflaged as the child grows up and develops, and through additional support within education and psychology.

Ironically children with Asperger's frequently create systems for themselves throughout all the different areas of their lives. With Cameron frequently the largest difficulty can be in communicating to him what behaviour was inappropriate and why! Asperger's children can be very capable when it comes to intellectually creating and developing strategies and rules to use to deal with/attempt to avoid the situation in future, just not necessarily at recognising the problem in the first place. For example they may still not notice a tense atmosphere in a room when they first walk in, but they will realise shortly by comparing behaviour and conversation to previous occasions when this happened, and then react accordingly. When Cameron gets really upset usually time has to be spent working out what he thinks the situation is before then trying to find a way to explain to him, in a form that he can understand, what the situation actually is.

What may surprise some is that a gifted student may still have learning difficulties. All too often gifted and special needs are seen at completely opposite ends of the scale. If we consider that we defined the difference between intelligent/bright/able and gifted as the presence of an aptitude that cannot be learnt, it is easy to see that you could, for example, have a gifted musician who had difficulties reading or writing. It would be wrong however to ignore their difficulties in favour of concentrating totally on their musical ability and any other areas that they might be succeeding in. This extends to not creating more challenges in their lives by pushing the child into education situations they aren't socially ready for, removing them from their peers, and the development opportunities that they offer, or by pushing them into an activity or discipline that they don't want to do. Having a difficulty and being gifted is more than sufficient challenge for any child, they don't need any more being added! Whether or not a child has a learning difficulty as well as being gifted doesn't fundamentally change anything; understanding their strengths and weaknesses and the necessity of supporting their development in a balanced way is still applicable. Any supporting mechanisms put in place need to address both the learning difficulty and the giftedness; neglecting one in favour of the other benefits no-one, especially not the child. There is a risk that if a child is gifted in a non-academic area but has a learning difficulty, all focus will move to developing their gift and their intellectual development will fall a poor second. Addressing the giftedness without considering the impact of the learning difficulty will cause frustration and de-motivation in school, while equally addressing the learning difficulty without looking at the giftedness will lead to boredom.

Dyslexia

Dyslexia can occur in any child, gifted or not. However unfortunately there are still those within education who have been known to argue against giftedness on this basis. This is an insulting stance to take, especially considering that within education circles IQ tests are judged to be the best way to assign a level to a child's intelligence. The effectiveness of this approach, or rather the weaknesses of it, were discussed in chapter 3 at length, however the point would be that the test most commonly used in the UK for gifted children is currently the WISC-IV. This test doesn't actually require a child to do any reading or writing. This means that the test has been deliberately designed to judge intelligence completely separately from reading and writing ability; that is to say that they are intentionally made irrelevant.

Any learning difficulties a child may have should not be seen as having any form of limiting affect on their academic potential; it will certainly cause some difficulties but with the right support and strategies in place these difficulties aren't insurmountable. This is the case whether they are gifted or not, although perhaps the vital phrase here is "the right support"!

Problems due to dyslexia can manifest themselves in a number of forms such as poor spelling, problems reading and poor short term memory. Identifying a child as gifted is more difficult where dyslexia is present; typically if their special abilities and gifts are intellectual they are often masked behind the symptoms of dyslexia. For parents there can often be a certain amount of confusion that the child they see at home who is verbally very bright and a hard worker, is finding it difficult to cope with the demands of written work at school and getting poor marks. Ultimately this can have a damaging effect on the child who upon seeing this disparity between themselves and their peers chooses to label themselves as "stupid" and loses interest in academic matters and essentially gives up. This disillusionment leads to poor classroom behaviour and underachievement.

Any child who struggles to express themselves on paper but who is clearly verbally bright and articulate needs to be identified and supported in implementing strategies to address the issues. Many people are against putting labels on children; however in the case of dyslexia it is often a relief to the children concerned to be able to understand these difficulties and come to the realisation that it is not related to their ability and potential, that they aren't stupid and that something can be done about it.

Dyspraxia

Dyspraxia is defined as an impairment or immaturity in regards to movement and co-ordination; it also affects making plans of action and how to carry them out. Although the problem isn't as widely recognised and understood as dyslexia, it is thought to affect up to ten per cent of the population at large, with boys more commonly affected than girls. Unfortunately the symptoms of dyspraxia often present as the complete opposite of key identifying factors for giftedness and it is therefore easy to see how much of a problem this can present. For example typically gifted children frequently reach developmental milestones early, whereas with dyspraxia they would be more likely to reach these milestones late. Frequently children with dyspraxia exhibit poor handwriting skills due to difficulty with motor skills although interestingly gifted children tend to have problems with handwriting in any case since, as many believe, the brain is processing information so quickly the body can't keep up! The key point however is this. In the case of dyspraxia there is a clear physical difficulty; for example problems gripping the pen, difficulty keeping to lines, problems forming letters. Some people with dyspraxia may also be over-sensitive to touch or have articulatory dyspraxia, which means they have difficulties with speaking and pronunciation. Dyspraxia can also overlap with dyslexia, ADD (Attention Deficit Disorder), ADHD (Attention Deficit Hyperactivity Disorder), Asperger's Syndrome and Dyscalculia (which is dealt with in the next section).

As with dyslexia, a child with dyspraxia will often feel frustrated and again the problem can lead to underachievement. Emotional support is essential to relieve the anxieties and maintain self-esteem.

Dyscalculia

Dyscalculia is defined as "a condition that affects the ability to acquire arithmetical skills". Those with dyscalculia find difficulty in understanding simple number concepts, struggle to grasp number in general and have problems in learning any facts involving numbers. An example would be that presented with 3 apples generally a child could instantly tell that there are 3 without having to count them, a child with dyscalculia isn't capable of this. From a simplistic viewpoint dyscalculia can be considered as "dyslexia for numbers", however unlike dyslexia the condition is still not widely understood and therefore is poorly diagnosed despite affecting 3-6% of the population. Currently there is no formal diagnostic test for dyscalculia although research is under way to rectify this. More than a small part of the problem is that no clear cause has yet been established. Dyscalculia should not be confused with acalculia, which is caused by some kinds of brain injury. Children who have dyslexia do not necessarily have dyscalculia and vice versa but it is possible to have both. In the end though the approach to this problem, in terms of emotional support and help, is no different from the advice given for dyslexia.

8 Enrichment Versus Acceleration

Having a child moving well beyond their peers, whether that be in one specific subject or generally across all subjects, throws up a fundamental problem; how should that ability be nurtured and encouraged. It is all very well racing ahead into more and more advanced material but the mistake should not be made in assuming that advancement through textbooks necessarily equates to understanding. For GCSE examinations, and to a lesser extent A-level examinations, it is more than possible to get good grades without truly understanding the material. The format of questions is so well defined that they can easily be predicted and therefore rehearsed; what is known as rote learning. It is therefore vital to consider enrichment and not just acceleration. Enrichment ensures that material is not just read but understood; its meaning is absorbed as well as learning how it fits in with other areas of study. Professor Arthur Aufderheide states that "All knowledge is connected to all other knowledge. The fun is in making the connections". Enrichment is going beyond the basic information needed just to pass exams, to the background of a topic and an expansion sideways of knowledge. It is only with this kind of proper understanding and grasp of a subject that it can be used outside of chasing achievements and put to practical use. The psychiatrist Dr. Roger Lewin once said "...too often we give our children answers to remember rather than problems to solve...".

When Cameron first started studying with the Open University he began by taking the course "The History of Maths". Whilst it was still a university level course, its content was as much, if not more, about enrichment than it was about acceleration. It gave him a knowledge about the development of Maths from around the ancient world, how the various theories came together and provided not just the names of those who had created the formulae and theories he had been working with but the backdrop to their discoveries, and details of the lives of the mathematicians themselves. This lead to Cameron going into his new school for the first time, looking at a Maths poster on the wall and announcing to his astonished teacher that Euler had come up that theory, and then going on to describe the circumstances surrounding the discovery! Knowing how theories were developed and the interactions that created the mathematics that exists today aids actual understanding.

The problem with a lot of the Maths in secondary education is that there is often a blind learning of facts and an expected acceptance of taught material without understanding how and why something is the case; therefore this particular Open University course explored where a lot of current thinking and understanding came from and the contributions that were made by different cultures. Cameron was never happy simply learning the plain facts to pass the exams. As with everything else he needed to know why, what the story was behind the work and had to be found tutors who could spend the necessary time discussing around the topic. In the high school environment, with a room full of pupils at different levels, all needing to be taught the material so that as many as possible achieve a pre-set level of success, and with a pre-defined curriculum, there simply isn't the time to go into any great depth.

Within the school environment it can often be the case that the best that can be offered is enrichment. A school may lack the facilities to take a child to the next level, especially if a child has advanced to the point where any further development would actually be beyond what the school can provide. Rather than looking to introduce new concepts and ideas, the school tends more to offer increasingly complex examples within the current topic, for example offering to teach Cameron the units of A-Level Maths that he had rejected when he was making study selections for his exam. Whilst this particular approach to enrichment caters for the brighter children in the class and can pose somewhat of a challenge, there comes a point where even this doesn't work. There are, after all, only so many ways to explore a topic before interest is lost and boredom sets in! It is especially true that enrichment is insufficient if the work at that level is too easy and unsatisfying for the child to study. There being more of it doesn't suddenly make the work more challenging!

Acceleration involves introducing work that would normally be reserved for someone in a higher year group. In an article written by the ERIC Clearing-house on Disabilities and Gifted Education in the United States it was noted "....the decision to allow a child to accelerate is one that must be made for each child, taking into account his or her intellectual and emotional needs....research about acceleration consistently documents positive effects, both academic and social, for children who have accelerated, but educators have been slow to embrace the option.". Of note is the reference to ensuring what is appropriate for a child's emotional needs and of how essential it is to tailor the solution to each individual. Again, there can be very real reasons why it is simply impossible for a school to offer advancement. However this isn't always the case and it isn't unknown for the issue to be more a case that the school is unwilling to put in the effort required to provide advancement. It may also be that a school can misinterpret a request for advancement as being either a slight on their teaching provision or as an example of parents pushing, in the most negative meaning of the term, at their children to achieve faster. Cameron's final two years of primary school involved round after round of meetings and delays during which we tried desperately to get something changed, while watching him become increasingly fed up with school and his behaviour deteriorating. Our requests were repeatedly rejected, most often with the statement that Cameron was already being stretched and doing all he was capable of. It is therefore both ironic and extremely annoying that after he went to high school where they did do something about his need for advancement that his primary school then tried to claim some of the credit for his achievements! The constant rejection of the need to advance Cameron, the unhappiness that it caused him and the amount of time and effort we spent fighting to get anyone in the primary system to take us seriously is still something we resent to this day. There was never any need for it to be that difficult.

When distance learning is brought into the mix the number of issues is reduced since the child is still able to retain the same environment for the development of their social and emotional skills. In a review provided for gifted students by Johns Hopkins University, Baltimore in 1994, Lesley MacKay commented that, "Acceleration's potential as an escape hatch from boredom is extremely important. The lack of challenge in school is not only tragic, it's damaging.". This makes blank refusals by schools to contemplate advancement even worse. They aren't just holding back a child's intellectual development, they are actually actively damaging it!" The National Association for Gifted Children (NAGC) in the UK had this to say, "Educational acceleration is one of the cornerstones of exemplary gifted education practices, with more research supporting this intervention than any other in the literature on gifted individuals.". This makes the continual ignoring of advancement a failure on the part of the education system. Presumably it is only if gifted children become so bored that they seriously disrupt classes or start playing truant that some schools may finally take action. After all, that's when they start damaging the average class grades and the school's attendance figures!

Acceleration can take a number of forms, for example:

- early admission to school

- skipping years in school e.g. going straight from year 1 to year 3

- "telescoping", the name given to reducing the amount of time taken to complete a key stage

- individual subject acceleration

- ability grouping of like-minded students

- mentoring at a one to one level by an expert in that subject

- early entry to university

Great care must be taken with acceleration that the intellectual development is not done at the expense of social and emotional development. For almost half of the examples above the option would require the child to be put into a peer group that they would otherwise not be in. In the case of early admission to school this may only be a matter of several months and therefore may not be of consequence but nonetheless is an important consideration. Many schools believe that the younger children starting their first school year should only be taking half days initially, out of concern that they may not be emotionally ready for the strain of a full day. In Cameron's case it was a rigid insistence on sticking to this policy that caused problems as he was dragged away reluctant and crying most days! In the case of those with Asperger's Syndrome however there is already a potential imbalance between the social, emotional and intellectual needs and care must be taken that this is not made worse. Advancing a child with Asperger's Syndrome so that they are surrounded by those who are only their peers intellectually is unlikely to do them any favours in the other areas of their development.

Ideally ability grouping of like-minded students is a good solution. Not only does it hopefully satisfy their intellectual needs but since the work is a shared experience it is not the lonely exercise it may otherwise have been. It allows development of social maturity to occur in the best place, among their peers. Ultimately of course this is only effective up to a point – at the higher levels of giftedness (moving through "best in set", "best in class", "best in school", "best in county"), a child becomes more and more separated from their peers in terms of having these shared learning experiences and the risks of neglecting the social and emotional needs seem to become more and more inevitable.

For many children purely concentrating on enrichment is entirely appropriate. It provides the appropriate challenge to alleviate boredom while at the same time ensuring a thorough and detailed understanding of the topic. Where enrichment on its own is insufficient in this regard, acceleration then provides that additional challenge. Great care must be taken to ensure that acceleration isn't done simply for the sake of it; that is to say that it is an absolutely necessary tool which going without would be more damaging than to have it. This comes back to the attitude, previously dealt with in Chapter 5, of treating learning like it is a race, as if the child earliest past the finishing post wins! That attitude can leave a child losing far more than they win, when their lives in the social and emotional arenas are judged. Acceleration needs be used alongside enrichment to ensure that the new material is truly understood. Remember that racing ahead doesn't automatically equate to understanding; it may be in areas that are more abstract, such as English, that there may be a need for a child to mature socially and emotionally before they can move any further ahead. It can be hard for anyone to intellectually analyse, or communicate across to others something that they aren't mature enough to grasp themselves.

There are some who see that a choice needs to be made between enrichment and acceleration, as if the two were mutually exclusive; that is simply not the case. At this point we would have to include, from personal experience, that a number of schools hold this belief. You can have enrichment without acceleration; you can't have acceleration without enrichment. Acceleration without enrichment will stall at some point when advancement suddenly tries to outstrip understanding.

Remember that enrichment is not simply "more of the same". It can hardly be considered enrichment that when your child completes 10 questions in class, they are given another 10 of the same kind! This is the so-called enrichment that Cameron kept encountering in primary school. It didn't help matters any because he was still bored and unfulfilled, just busier in class and leaving the teacher alone! It ultimately didn't improve his restless and disruptive behaviour in class, with his efforts to attract attention damaging his relationships with other children, who were understandably fed up with having their work disrupted. In this case failure to accelerate one child was actually having a negative effect on an entire classroom! Enrichment takes the topic deeper and broader, it shouldn't simply repeat it.

Where a child advances into degree level material additional challenges start to arise. At this level it is not simply a matter of answering a black and white question which is either right or wrong but rather having to think, explore and explain approaches. These more advanced approaches are skills that are introduced from other disciplines. There is an assumption that someone studying one subject at degree level will have studied other subjects that dove-tail with that one up to at least GCSE, if not A-Level. One example of this would be when we had to get in a

Physics tutor for a couple of sessions because Cameron's Maths studies were now relying on physics knowledge that he simply hadn't encountered when just over 2 years into his high school education!

When Cameron moved on to study second year degree level material (Open University Level 2 courses), which was a more detailed study within a narrower area of Mathematics, it was no longer sufficient to just be able to understand what was being asked and then provide an answer; Cameron was required to show true understanding, detailed working out and an ability to communicate ideas effectively. At this point additional skills were needed that at his age had not yet been developed particularly, for example, in essay writing. With his Maths vastly outstripping all his other academic studies, this was bound to happen. We had to ask ourselves whether we would pause his advancement or whether he should take the chance to improve his other skills. This was an important lesson for all concerned that no subject can be taken successfully to a high level without developing good communication skills. Cameron had to learn the skill of transferring the knowledge in his head to the paper. The decision to allow Cameron to progress to third year degree material (Level 3) was again the subject of much care and a watchful eye was kept on Cameron by the Open University to ensure that he was ready for that leap.

For Cameron one of the big motivators to him was clearly defined targets. GCSE, A-Level and Open University courses represented easily defined goals that he could work towards rather than work in a vague way. Each course was a tangible achievement and he knew where he was, what was expected of him and what he had to complete. To a certain extent this need for clearly delineated goals and structures is a trait of Asperger's Syndrome; that black and white thinking that needs everything to be clearly defined and part of a clearly understood system, a completely logical progression.

Whether it be via distance learning, or a conventional university, the university student is expected to be able to motivate themselves and manage their time effectively to meet the demands of submitting test papers and submitting assignments. This isn't something that most children have mastered in their early teens, it is something that is gradually developed in the run up to GCSEs. Parents who send their children to university seem to neglect the additional study skills that are necessary to truly succeed. Also there is a tendency amongst parents who send their children to university to micro-manage their studies in general. This will no longer be possible when they are in university and they have not had the chance to develop self-discipline and their own organisational skills because someone else has been doing it for them all so far.

Caution must be shown that for bright children the expectations that are set are not unreasonably high, or that the expectations that others have of them are nothing like their own. For children that have proven their aptitude for a subject it is also all too easy for them to set a benchmark for themselves which others will then expect them to maintain or even exceed. Whether it be enrichment or acceleration, children need to have activities both at home and in school which allow them to stretch their minds using creative thinking and problem-solving skills. They also need to still be enjoying the process and getting satisfaction from it. There also needs to be a flexible approach taken to advancing any child's studies of being prepared to change a course of action should it no longer be working.

Enrichment should not be seen as something that is solely the responsibility of the school. Children frequently have a thirst for knowledge that cannot simply be turned off at the end of the school day, they are desperate to continue learning. Schools may not be in a position to offer any enrichment and also it may be more appropriate for the form of enrichment to not be classroom based. Families can support enrichment in a variety of extra-curricular and non-academic ways such as exploring practical applications of skills and visiting museums and other places of interest. This can help lift their studies beyond the purely theoretical and enhance the child's interest by helping make their studies come alive for them.

When parents and teachers work together and can agree on a common goal, gifted children can reach tremendous heights in fulfilling their potential. Sadly this isn't always possible for various reasons including lack of resources, lack of time and lack of willingness to make any effort for whatever reason. Most importantly though it is vital that it is the children themselves who are given the opportunity to explore their special talents. It is for the parents and teachers to ensure that the children are nurtured, encouraged and gently guided in a direction that is suitable for them; in making sure that they have access to stimulating resources and where possible are able to interact with peers with whom they can share their intellectual interests or artistic pursuits. This is all supposed to be for the child's benefit, not to create reflected glory for either parents or schools to bask in. As the Psychologist Dr Peter Congden (and expert in the field of giftedness in the UK) said of gifted children, "Sometimes they are being exploited by their parents, who are living their lives and ambitions through their children." Both groups have responsibilities towards the child; everything is easier for all parties and more can be achieved if they are following the same course of action and are content in doing so! It can only be through acceptance, understanding and guidance that these children will be able to fully develop into happy and fulfilled adults.

9 Managing Expectations

When a child finds something so easy to them that the expectation, both from them and possibly from others, is for full marks every time then there are going to be problems. They begin to see this as the way it is supposed to be. As we have mentioned previously, all throughout junior school we can look back to Cameron's Maths books and it would be difficult to find any questions he got wrong, even with any of the so-called enrichment material that was (sometimes) provided, leaving the unanswered, to this day, question of why this wasn't enough reason for any of his teachers to think that maybe this work was too easy. This can be quite a common problem for gifted children, that they can know more than half of a curriculum before the academic year even starts. This inevitably leads to boredom as they have to go over the material again at the same pace as the rest of the class.

As the years passed 100% became the norm for Cameron and anything less by him was deemed to be a failure in his eyes. It also seemed to lead many of his teachers to believe that it wasn't particularly necessary to spend any time or effort on his Maths skills presumably because he was in absolutely no danger of failing. Of course this isn't quite true. He wasn't in any danger of failing there and then, however the same couldn't be said for in the future as his frustration at essentially spinning his wheels increased. There was always the risk that he would, as many other gifted children before him have done, decide that it wasn't worth caring any more and to simply stop trying, rejecting the school system.

The idea of pushing Cameron any further or higher was repeatedly raised by us as a possibility and just as repeatedly rejected. At this point we already knew Cameron was capable of Maths several years more advanced than what he was working on in school. We had had suspicions for some time which had led us, when he was 8, to ask a Maths tutor we knew to check what he was actually capable of doing. When we returned at the end of the session she said that he had successfully sailed through a Maths test for 11 year olds. It was also slightly puzzling at the time that Cameron generally got full marks in Maths and, on the odd occasion that he didn't, it wasn't the difficult questions that he lost marks on. Rather it was the easy ones and he usually lost marks due to rushing, to not paying attention and then making silly mistakes. Two separate primary schools denied on several occasions that Cameron's needs weren't being met and then stated that he was doing the most advanced work he was capable of already. Of course in less than a year from us last being told that, Cameron was taking his Maths and Additional Maths GCSEs and finding them incredibly easy.

Many gifted children however tend to have problems with test-taking, with their impatience with the work leading them to skip over instructions for tests or omitting vital steps in reaching the correct answer. A gifted child can often also think in such an abstract way that they become confused by multiple choice questions; over thinking and viewing the question from so many angles that they feel they can justify every answer option! Just because a child is gifted doesn't mean that they don't have any problems that need extra attention!

The expectation of teachers is often that what they are teaching children is sufficiently advanced for them, as it is designed to be, and that to progress quicker is unnecessary. Perhaps part of the problem is that so much focus is placed on children who have difficulty keeping up or who are unwilling to learn. There is absolutely no question that these are important issues that must be dealt with but that doesn't mean that those who can, and should, be moving on faster should be ignored! Ironically enforcing the expectation that a gifted child should be happy with what everyone else is working on could well turn them into one of the children unwilling to learn! There is also the expectation that any parents pushing for their child to be moving to more advanced material are just trying to get their child to achieve faster and that it is not in the best interests of the child.

In this day and age teachers and schools have to constantly meet targets regarding the grades they achieve, and what percentage of pupils get them. These targets were designed to prevent schools from failing pupils and to make available for all children a free, high standard education. It was supposed to mean that everyone had the best chance possible at leaving school with a decent level of education. It was never supposed to become an exercise in chasing statistics, which is what it can become. This is another set of expectations, just one placed on a school by the education board and parents, and on teachers by headteachers and parents.

Ideally, all children will be challenged appropriately; their work neither too hard nor too easy. It is this balance that is referred to in professional circles as the "zone of proximal development". The problem with finding this "zone" is that children all have their individual strengths and weaknesses and that is even without considering those who are gifted or those who could be considered to have any kind of "special needs"!

If the work that is set is too hard then often children will simply give up, believing themselves incapable of meeting the demands of the subject. They worry that it will be too stressful and it will be boring – why from a child's point of view continue with something that you don't feel you are good at, keep embarrassing yourself trying to do and for which you can't get the right answers? Continuing doing their best and failing with material that others are succeeding at, but that they can't even fully grasp, is depressing for anyone, never mind for children. Goals must be believable and achievable!

On the other hand when it comes to work that is too easy a child can and often does lose interest in the subject; it is not challenging and is therefore boring. A 2003 study suggested that, "It is surprising that very highly gifted children do not rebel more frequently against the inappropriate educational provision which is generally made for them. Studies have repeatedly found that the great majority of highly gifted students are required to work, in class, at levels several years below their tested achievement. Underachievement may be imposed on the exceptionally gifted child through the constraints of an inappropriate and undemanding educational programme or, as often happens, the child may deliberately underachieve in an attempt to seek peer-group acceptance." That is not to say that they won't get high marks but if a child has an interest in a subject then marks are not the only consideration; their interest should be encouraged, nurtured and developed. They need to feel that they are learning and to see progress as well as getting success in the form of great results. Paradoxically younger children who find work too easy and therefore find it difficult to concentrate, and lack the vocabulary to explain the problem, may in fact convince themselves and others that the work is too difficult for them! This is why teachers and parents need to keep a careful eye on children's progress, achievements and abilities. It is also why it is essential to keep an open mind! Cameron's primary school teachers were so determined that advancing his Maths was the wrong course of action that they not only ignored any other possibilities but also refused to contemplate that their actions might be causing his behavioural issues. The school had no higher expectations when it came to Maths of Cameron than that he would continue to achieve his near perfect scores in the subject. As he was a student who was successful, taking high grades as the only measurement of success, they wanted to leave the situation alone and concentrate on those who weren't getting good marks. That Cameron was capable of doing so much more was to them totally unimportant! It is a pity in the current fashion to met government targets that sometimes the actual individual, and the fact that maybe they could dramatically outstrip the targets, is forgotten.

With many gifted children it is clear the issue is not that the work is too hard. Indeed without identification, intervention and additional support the child may sail through school with the highest grades, but sooner or later there will inevitably be a point, either in their school life, in university or in later employment that they will come across something that doesn't come easily. That is not to say that they are incapable of doing the work, but because they have never been challenged in this way, that they actually have to put in effort, that they simply don't know how to approach this bump in the road. While all their peers have learnt the lessons of self-discipline and of how to have the persistence to keep going when the work gets difficult, they won't know how to deal with it. They could be put off, deciding that they can no longer go any further, or just be totally shocked and need someone to guide them through it. Cameron found the idea of actually having to occasionally think about his Maths work a complete surprise as he had spent most of his primary school career coasting through the material with little to no effort. This doesn't produce a good work ethic! While GCSE and A-Level material was still horribly easy for him, he did have to learn new concepts and put some effort into learning new methods of working and this was an experience that he hadn't had for years!

The idea that he might actually make the odd mistake was also something that Cameron struggled to accept. This might seem surprising but not if viewed from the point of view of any high achieving child who has spent years getting near-perfect marks. This becomes the norm for them and they come to see this as the way life works; that the work is easy and they virtually always get full marks. For them it is unacceptable to achieve anything less. Neither us nor Cameron's primary teachers could understand why he was so upset when he made Maths mistakes, going as far once to burst into tears in the middle of class, when he was aged about 9 or 10, for getting 59 out of 60! What was a complete over-reaction from our viewpoint is understandable from his, especially as gifted children can be emotionally sensitive. The problem is that any attitude or opinion, especially that of a child, that has time to become entrenched is hard to change. When Cameron started into the accelerated work and began to make mistakes it took us some time to grasp how large this problem was. It became clear that even if Cameron understood logically that he could make mistakes, it was a lot harder for him to actually truly believe it. He thought that anyone who was any good at Maths would be beyond getting anything wrong, which may seem childish but after all he was an emotionally immature 11 year old when he started doing his accelerated work! We had to explain to him that even Maths Professors in universities, exalted beings from Cameron's perspective, were allowed, and often do make, mistakes. While his expectations of personal perfection aren't quite as bad as they were he still drives himself to be perfect and is far too hard on himself. There is an aspect of the black and white thinking associated with Asperger's Syndrome coming into play slightly in this for him though as well, because everything is either a success or failure, there is no in-between, or grey area!

Many assume that a gifted child who is capable of understanding work at a much higher level than their peers will naturally move through exams. Just because a child is a high achiever doesn't mean that they won't have to work hard for exam success, after all understanding the work in class isn't the same as presenting it in the necessary form expected in an exam. Cameron knew the material but had to be taught how to read the question so that he understood what knowledge he was being asked to use and prove he knew. He also had to be taught the needed study skills as he moved through different levels of study and of how to prepare for exams.

It is a myth to think that gifted children are always the bright-eyed, bushy-tailed eager students in the classroom, hanging on every word spoken by the teacher and enjoying homework. Although this can be the case with some gifted children it is certainly not typical behaviour and it is unlikely to be sustained. Any child who behaves like that is an enthusiastic pupil, most likely very bright, and no doubt a joy to have from a teacher's perspective! However many gifted children behave in quite the opposite manner, presented as inattentive, careless and neglecting to do homework. This is another illustration of one of the differences between bright and gifted. Bright children can remain challenged and interested by progressing at the typically developing pace with some enrichment material provided but gifted children may not.

When dealing with gifted children one of the most common issues parents can face is that of disorganisation. Just because a child has an academic aptitude and a memory for facts it in no way means that they are able to perform day to day tasks well. Often gifted children are more interested in their own passions then they are in the monotony of daily life. Albert Einstein once famously got so distracted by his own thoughts that he actually forgot where he lived! Ultimately the problem can reach such a level that the child under-performs at school through, for example, lack of revision skills or failure to complete and hand in homework. As their teachers only see children in a very narrow context, it falls to the parents to help their children learn organisation skills. Often these skills don't come easily and teaching them can involve a lot of frustration, however with persistence progress can be made. Rather than worry about everything at once, it's really a simple case of concentrating on one thing at a time and dealing with things in bite-size chunks.

Not all gifted children have this problem; in fact some are the complete opposite, obsessively organised and completely inflexible to interruptions of systems and routines. Irrespective of in which extreme a child may lie, the solution in both cases is the same. Calmly explain what is and is not expected of them without being critical. Get them to engage with the process and recognise the benefits of sorting the issue out; for example less arguments with parents, reduced frustration, better results. One word of caution though; these problems should never hold a gifted child back as appropriate skills will come in time!

For the majority of children starting school, school was something that was looked forward to and is enjoyable and interesting. Most children view starting school as a great adventure. Notwithstanding the fact that some children are better behaved than others, very few children start their school lives with no interest in learning; to learn new things and to expand on what they already know. The problems arise for gifted children when information that is being taught to them is things they already know and lessons move from being enjoyed to being endured. Adults don't enjoy being told what they already know, why should children with their lower boredom threshold be content to put up with it! Such problems run the risk of the child becoming so used to daydreaming through the repetitive part of lessons that it actually becomes a habit that spreads into other classes and even other areas of their life, which is exactly what happened with Cameron. Even if a lesson is presenting material that is new to the child, they may find that the information is absorbed quickly and the lesson becomes boring while time is spent reinforcing the ideas to ensure they are learnt by the rest of the class. Cameron used to lose interest before teachers had even finished the explanation and repeated examples for the whole class of what Maths they were doing that day. What adult can honestly say they would be happy to listen attentively to over 10 minutes of explanation of something they understood in the first minute? This is what can be expected of gifted children though and frankly asks for more self-control than young children are generally capable of having!

It is a simple and established fact that gifted children who are not challenged in school may end up becoming underachievers. To them it is easier to give up than to have to deal with suffering mind-numbing boredom day after day. Ultimately this can mean they also find it difficult to meet the challenges later in life that lead to success. Cameron began school as highly enthusiastic and bursting to learn more but by the time he was in the sixth year of primary school those days were gone! It had become so easy it was boring and not worth getting excited about which, combined with the fact he was "different", a common problem for either gifted or Asperger's children, resulted in him being bullied which meant that he had to frequently be told that going to school wasn't up for debate! Of course as detailed above it didn't even take until Cameron was in the world of work before he had to learn to adjust to being fallible! While it's unfortunate that he developed this skewed view of the world in the first place, long term it is better that it is being dealt with while he is still a child living at home and before he becomes an adult!

Finding work too easy is not just an intellectual issue. The challenges of everyday work brings about interaction with their social and intellectual peers who discuss, exchange ideas, complain and in this way can often solve problems. It eliminates a perfect chance to develop the skill of working in groups, as in class groups are boring to the child who already knows the answer and thinks the work is too easy. They won't make themselves very popular either if they let slip that they think it is too simple as that implies they think the rest of the group is stupid! Discussing schoolwork outside the classroom is a common source of social interaction with peers as schoolwork is the one thing that they should all have in common! With their experience of the schoolwork so radically different from those around them this point of contention is another way for them to not quite fit in, causing further problems with social development.

There appears to be a firm expectation in many schools that advancing a gifted child will damage their social development by the act of giving them a different academic experience. This is the wrong way round as they are already different from those around them, in the same way that those struggling with academic expectations are different. Different is, after all, the very definition of special but nobody would think of arguing that no efforts should be made to help those who are falling behind due to Special Needs. Yet it is suddenly completely different if they are at the other end of the spectrum! As with children who are struggling, it is when they are receiving the provision that helps them achieve their potential, improving their attitude and as a result their behaviour, that they will best fit in!

Mathematics to Cameron only started to present a sufficient challenge once he was well into his degree. It was never the intention to go this far; the idea was to allow him to move ahead until the point where he was being stretched and challenged. When Cameron's teacher gave him full access to material up to the top level of GCSE Maths for over the Christmas holidays it wasn't anyone's expectation that he would finish it. Even then no-one could envisage how far ahead beyond even that his ability would take him. That he would move ahead through 5 years of work in 4 months never occurred to anyone involved. There were no ultimate expectations, everyone was just trying to figure out what it was that Cameron actually needed and then sort out how to provide it! In this case the expectations of both us, as his parents, and the school had to be radically altered as we all realised that they were far below what they should be for him! It isn't just high expectations that can be damaging; low expectations are bad for a child's self-esteem and run the danger of becoming self-fulfilling.

Even now it is not the Maths that is the challenge for Cameron but being forced to show the working out and explain every step that was used in getting to the final answer. The more logical expectation, and the one held by most people if they know he is having difficulties, is that he has reached the limit of his current abilities. Yet it isn't understanding the work or getting the right answers that is giving Cameron the issues. Progressing through GCSE, A-Level and into degree level work there are less and less marks given just for stating the final answer; it is more than possible to get only 50% on a test paper where every final answer is correct. In common with many children in this situation, Cameron typically demonstrates A-D rather than A-B-C-D processes in his work, skipping entire steps in his written answers.

It is in this that we start to see one of the differences between a child who is very bright/intelligent and one who would be considered "gifted". For a child who is bright and has learnt solely through books, it is relatively easy to be able to present answers in the way that was taught and any deviation may well be a case of laziness and taking short cuts! The gifted child however possesses an ability that cannot be purely taught and is often able to see things in a way that other people cannot. There are two main types of learners amongst gifted children; "mappers", also known as sequential learners, and "leapers", or spatial learners. Leapers make leaps in their logic, these children can't always say how they got an answer as they often leave out important steps in reaching the answer, even in their own heads. This is in contrast to mappers who learn everything in steps but can become so focused on the stages which work up to the answer that they get lost in the detail before they reach the answer.

They haven't achieved their progress purely from study, there is an innate ability coming deeply into play which means they can just see the answer. This should not be interpreted as laziness; on more than one occasion Cameron has been asked to explain how he got from one thing to another and, with a bewildered look, his reply often is "it just is". Indeed there have been occasions where an answer has been given (correctly) where

Cameron genuinely doesn't know how he got to that answer; to him "it just is". He has serious difficulty in writing down the steps in between because, in his own head, there weren't any, he instinctively knew the answer. Explaining properly and consistently step-by-step is an expectation Cameron is going to have to learn to meet sooner or later if he wants to continue, because presenting work in a way that others can follow becomes vital at tertiary level.

10 The Future

For any parent it is hard not to think ahead to the future, wanting our children to have the things that we perhaps didn't have or to give them opportunities that maybe weren't available to us. We want them to have a happy childhood while at the same time succeeding in everything they undertake, to achieve their full potential and grow up to be happy adults. Whether we want them to have better teachers, an easier time socially or to be talented in sport, either because we were or weren't, every parent inevitably brings a certain amount of their own bias to the table. What is important is to use those drives for your child's benefit but not to the extent where parents overrun the desires of their child.

A number of years ago we took our daughter, Bethany, to some ballet classes since she had become somewhat obsessed through watching dancers on TV and we wanted to see if we could find a physical activity to get her moving, especially as Cameron often didn't want to play outside with her! After a couple of weeks we couldn't stand the environment any more; whilst Bethany practically skipped in for classes which she was looking forward to, some of the other children were (and in one case literally) forced in. We witnessed parents who were so convinced that their child was destined for the life of a professional dancer that they would argue with the instructor and with other parents to the point where it became almost a physical altercation. Frankly we didn't feel that it was beneficial for her to be placed in such a negative environment and in the company of obsessive parents and pressurised children. She very quickly found for herself that what she had expected bore no resemblance to the reality of the situation! Instead we kept our eyes open and decided to try Karate as a family activity to get us all fit and teach Cameron to defend himself a bit. Both children, in their own very different ways, took to it like ducks to water and we never looked back!

In 2004 Prince Charles made a statement that raised a lot of controversy at the time. Part of his speech was, "Why do they (people today) all seem to think they are qualified to do things far beyond their technical capabilities? This is to do with the learning culture in schools as a consequence of child-centred system which admits no failure. People think they can all be pop stars, High Court judges, brilliant TV personalities or infinitely more competent heads of state without ever putting in the necessary work or having natural ability." There appears to be an attitude of entitlement today where people feel that the world owes them. From people who spend all their time blaming anyone and everyone for their problems while doing nothing about it to the young people obsessed with respect and the way they are constantly convinced they aren't getting enough of it. Sports Days aren't held or, when they are, they aren't competitive in case someone gets upset. Whilst it is true that it isn't only the winning that's important, the taking part only counts if there is actually going to be a winner! The proverb is supposed to be about learning how to accept losing or winning gracefully - an important social lesson to learn. If no one wins then all that the children learn at these events is how to run around while a lot of people cheer at them!

Great achievement requires 2 things; talent and hard work and even then that doesn't guarantee success but it certainly shortens the odds. This is what was bothering Prince Charles; that many children and young people have deeply unrealistic expectations. However he doesn't blame them as they have been led by the media and the school system, for example the non-event Sports Day, to believe that failure isn't a possibility. Within the school system this is because some schools have become so concerned with damaging children's self-esteem that they have hopelessly high self-esteem that has no basis in reality. The media relentlessly pumps out the success stories without ever mentioning that for every person who makes it, for example as a Premier League footballer with expensive cars and a million pound mansion, there are many thousands of people who didn't. Those footballers who make it to the top had natural ability, trained long and hard and made sacrifices to get there. When celebrating the great successes people often forget the years of hard work that came before the success and, for anyone at the top of their field, the continuing hard work involved in staying there!

This lack of reality deeply concerned Princes Charles who, after all, set up the Prince's Trust specifically to help those disadvantaged young people out there with talent and energy by offering mentoring support, training courses and small grants to give the best chance at success for those willing to use those tools to get it! He is simply concerned that there are young people out there, wasting their lives, chasing a dream that they don't have the ability to possibly achieve.

As we have said before, we live in a society that tells children that they can achieve whatever they want, be whoever they want but quite simply that just isn't true. It is only true within certain limits. With the right amount of effort and ability then maybe, but many career paths require an ability or perhaps "giftedness" to be able to succeed as a career; singer, dancer, footballer for example. If someone has no co-ordination, or sense of rhythm then regardless of how much they want it or how hard they work they aren't going to be a successful dancer. Genius may well be 99% perspiration but there is still that 1% inspiration! After all that was said by Thomas Edison the man who, to paraphrase, declared that he had never failed when trying to create the lightbulb, he had just found several thousand ways not to make one! That certainly shows determination but also that he wasn't afraid of hard work, in addition to the fact that even geniuses have to make an effort!

Someone can also be gifted but still fail to gain any great progress because they weren't willing to put in the effort. It doesn't matter how talented for example, at horse-riding a child might be, if they aren't willing to put in the hours of practice, looking after the horse and travelling to, and taking part in, competitions then they won't realise their potential or reach the heights of success that they could have. To quote Thomas Edison again, "Opportunity is missed by most people because it is dressed in overalls and looks like work"!

Even with the necessary ability some fields are so competitive that success is as much about luck as anything else. An example would be that in sports it can depend on a child being seen by a talent scout when they are on form, of being offered the right placement to develop their natural ability, to then get the right offers to move on, to take part in the right competitions or games and to be successful when they do so. It can mean a lot of being in the right place at the right time and avoiding misfortune. Many an athlete has had their career ended by accidental injury. Of course the drive to succeed means that one failure doesn't mean the end of any dreams of success. Gordon Ramsay severely damaged the cartilage in his knee when training at football, at a time when he was hoping to be signed for Glasgow Rangers Junior team, but he certainly didn't allow that to destroy any chance he had of success!

To encourage a child in something they enjoy but don't have an aptitude for as being a potential career path is not good parenting; it is irresponsible and setting them up for failure in the future. It is up to the parents and family to encourage a child to pursue a career not just in what they want to do but in what they are also actually capable of doing. It isn't enough to really want to do something and to be prepared to work really hard to get it, there has to be natural aptitude to build on. That is not to say children should not be encouraged in something that is of interest to them as a hobby – one doesn't need to be good at something to enjoy it! The key point being made here is the false hope of a successful career. Previous reference was made to talent shows such as "X-Factor" and

"Britain's Got Talent" and to the tone deaf teenagers who have convinced themselves they will be the next big thing in the music industry. These individuals certainly didn't lack self-belief, determination or the right attitude to achieve success but it was wasted due to the fact that they simply couldn't sing! That their loved ones didn't think to tell them isn't a kindness. There are two probable outcomes to this situation; either someone will at some point rudely disillusion them or they will continue to waste their lives chasing an unattainable goal. When Pete Waterman was on the panels for these shows he defended his treatment of the tone deaf by pointing out that he was telling them the truth, that they were wasting their lives, when they could and should be doing something else. Encouraging a child is one thing but that doesn't mean that it should be at the expense of honesty in terms of ability where appropriate.

Cameron's sister Bethany enjoys singing and has been involved in many school choirs over the years. She thoroughly enjoyed performing with her friends and worked hard, attending every practice and making sure she knew the songs perfectly, even listening to them continually during the car journey to school. As parents we encouraged her interest in the subject, we applauded her effort and enthusiasm but would we have been doing her any favours to tell her she was capable of something she was not? Several years ago Bethany spoke of being a pop star and we were quick to point out in a sensitive way that that is not where her strengths lay. She is good enough to sing in a primary school choir but will never have a good enough voice for anything further. She still enjoys to sing but now she is under no illusion that a career lies elsewhere! Bethany once tried out for a solo singing part in the school pantomime, without mentioning it to us first. We knew immediately, as parents whose support for their child's self-esteem hadn't rendered them deaf, that there was no way she had got the part. Our concern at being asked to speak to the Headteacher that afternoon turned to amusement when we realised that it was for the purpose of letting us, not Bethany, down gently that she hadn't got the part. We quickly reassured the poor man that while we were her ever-loving parents, we were still aware of her limitations, which actually surprised him! This serves to illustrate a rather disturbing trend. When we went to school children would be told outright that they hadn't got a part and it would have been the expectation that most parents wouldn't question that. Now failure to be judged good enough to sing a solo is broken carefully, not just to the child, but to their parents with the expectation that they may not take the news well. The last time Bethany was cast for a school production she was absolutely delighted to get the second largest part as the narrator because, as she said herself, she was never going to get the lead which went to her friend who can sing solos and is a talented actress. Bethany has a realistic view of her own abilities which allows her to be thrilled at coming second and also delighted for her friend; in other words a completely healthy attitude!

In helping a child prepare for the future they must learn what their own strengths and weaknesses are and this can only be done through varied experiences as they grow up. There can be a false impression that gifted children have a grand plan in their heads and already know where they are going in life. Children need to be encouraged to try out a range of interests and activities. Even if what they find out is that they hate something and are completely useless at it, that is still progress as they now know more than they did before! As long as children have a healthy attitude to failure then it will never be a waste of time, as any failure will be a valuable learning experience. It is also true that just because a child turns out to be naturally talented in one area that this doesn't mean it should be assumed that either this is their only talent! Just because Cameron is good at Maths, this doesn't mean that all other avenues should be closed; as good as he is at Maths perhaps there is something he is even better at? This is another case of where over specialisation at an early job can be damaging because it limits options unnecessarily. Also, as stated above, it may be that a child will find something that they will never make a career from but that they enjoy and could well be a life long hobby, which is far from worthless.

In recent years schools have introduced the notion in some situations that there is no such thing as "winners" and "losers", the most blatant example being the non-competitive Sports Days. Sorry, but that isn't how the world works! If childhood is preparation for life, why do people adapt situations in a way that doesn't reflect real life. In the real world there are winners and losers, and the skill of learning to be a gracious winner or loser needs to be learnt. Even when still in the school situation nobody appreciates someone who insists on revelling in their success or who deals badly with any failures they may have. It is in childhood that these skills are supposed to be learnt, after all that is why being a bad loser is thought of as a habit people "grow out of"! The less childhood reflects real life, the bigger the problems typically seen in adulthood. A child can still have an enjoyable childhood and be prepared for adolescence and adulthood.

For any parent there is really only one desire for their children in the future; that they are happy. Career prospects, wealth, qualifications are unimportant if the person isn't happy. Real happiness takes more than a successful career and wealth, something that should have been amply demonstrated by now by decades of the music industry, notably by Elvis, who was clearly not made happy by what he achieved. If we were asked to choose whether we would rather Cameron were an unhappy Maths

Professor or a happy road sweeper, we would have to choose the happy road sweeper. Of course that is not to say that we wouldn't feel disappointed to a certain extent because we believe he is capable of a lot more but if it didn't make him happy he has the choice to not pursue that avenue. It is ultimately Cameron's life and his to live the way he wants. As Dr. Mary Calderone (the Director of Planned Parenthood) wrote "Our children are not going to be just our children - they are going to be other people's husbands and wives and the parents of our grandchildren". We can only do our best for him while he is growing up to make the best choices possible and hope that we have provided him with enough resources to go out into the world and make the best life he can for himself. Parents have to accept that their children are individuals free to make their own choices and mistakes, while still being there to offer love and support for their children to fall back on.

In considering these desires for career prospects, prosperity etc., it should be recognised that these are very much materialistic values. The ambitions held for and by children should not just be about material possessions but go deeper. Despite all the gaudy signs of success consistently splashed across magazines and front pages by the media, that is not what success means. Real success is so much more than that; what could be more important than being successful as a caring, happy, confident human being who loves and is loved?

If we look deeper at why we desire lots of material possessions for our children, or even ourselves, it would be fair to say that the desire is not for things themselves but rather the satisfaction and happiness that is expected to be gained from them. Most of the things that people automatically associate with success are exactly that, just things, merely material trappings. There is an expectation that anyone who lives without worries about money and has is able to live in whatever way they choose will have happiness just magically turn up as part of the deal. If nothing else perhaps the divorce rates among the rich and famous, and the dirty laundry that is aired during divorce proceedings, should be proof that rich doesn't equal happy. Simply what we should want for children is not the symbols of happiness and contentment but happiness and contentment themselves.

Unfortunately the education system is primarily focused on teaching a child almost superficial skills and not developing that child as a well rounded person and ultimately a successful human being. There are classes in other world religions and cultures but does learning about the mechanics of how they function teach a child tolerance? My child may know what 2+2 is but do they understand compassion? They may know how to read but do they understand right from wrong?

Why don't schools teach children life skills and help them learn and understand themselves and others? Education gives facts; but why doesn't it teach how to concentrate? How to be a good husband or wife? How to be a good parent? How to live a balanced life?

However not all the responsibility for this lack of knowledge can be laid at the feet of teachers. After all there is a responsibility for parents and families to teach these concepts to children. A frequent lament from parents is about why schools aren't teaching their children respect. Perhaps the problem lies not as much with the teachers as with their parents. Children learn quickly by example and if they learn from their parents to have no respect for authority figures then a teacher with an entire class to teach may be fighting a losing battle. This is especially true if they don't respect their own parents through either their parents not being good role models, even from the point of view of their own children, or by not getting any respect from their parents, as respect is not a one way street. Many young people are left wondering why they aren't getting shown enough respect for their taste, at the same time as not showing any to anyone else!

The idea that somehow children are incapable of concentration is something that is perpetuated by the media. Television programmes have constant reminders of what was on just before the advert break, everything is presented in shorter and shorter segments and parents are constantly being told that they absolutely have to come up with things for their bored offspring to do during the holidays. When did children become unable to amuse themselves? If there are no longer any opportunities for them to have to exercise their concentration for any length of time or to have to fall back on their own resources then how exactly how are they going to develop their concentration skills? Lack of concentration in children risks becoming a self-fulfilling prophecy!

Schools try to do their part in teaching children social and emotional skills but their primary purpose is an academic education and they only have children for about 30 hours a week. What children do the rest of the time also has to be considered if anyone is looking at any areas of development where they are found to be lacking. They need to be mixing with other children and learning to develop their moral and ethical code from those around them. People bemoan the lack of a sense of community but don't ever volunteer their services and wonder why the next generation around them isn't keen to give up their time to help others. Our own parents took part in community events, we have taken part in running community events and children's camps with our children present and helping and now both Cameron and Bethany are keen to get involved and help others. They both help other people with their homework, stand up for other people who are being bullied, have run school fair stalls and both spent several years representing Prestatyn as Carnival Royals, attending community events and doing fundraising in all weathers! They have both become rather altruistic and all three children are known for having bright, sunny personalities!

Parents need to recognise the difference between acquiring knowledge and acquiring wisdom. Many people in this day and age have a lot of knowledge but very little wisdom. Someone once said "Knowledge is the understanding that a tomato is a fruit...wisdom is the understanding that you don't put tomatoes in fruit salads". In other words knowledge is the awareness and understanding of facts, truths or information, whereas wisdom is the ability to be able to apply that knowledge.

11 From The Horses Mouth!

Central to everything that we have done has been making sure that it was always the best thing for Cameron. We kept checking how he felt and it was his unhappiness, and how the way he was behaving in school was becoming so out of character, that led us to start pushing at his schools to take action. As time passed his behaviour got worse and he started saying he was too ill to go to school most mornings, which led us to demanding more and more that action be taken by them. Therefore high school, coming as it did after the mixed report from primary school which gave him outstanding remarks while voicing disappointment that he wasn't meeting his potential, was hoped to be a fresh start. This is exactly what it proved to be and was the first of many steps along the right road.

There has been no grand master plan that we were following and everything that we did was based on constantly assessing how it was working. Whenever one strategy failed, or when circumstances changed and something no longer worked, we looked around and tried again; we had to be prepared for change no matter how difficult it might be. But how did Cameron feel through this whole process? We felt that it was important that we should include Cameron's thoughts and feelings, as these were always central to decisions, on his experiences in his own words.

I remember back in my final primary school when I was about 9 years old finding the mathematics that was assigned to us by the curriculum very easy while every one of my peers found it difficult. I didn't understand why they thought it was difficult because it wasn't. Whenever I finished the work first some of them began to call me names first by "nerd" or "scrawny" and then they started to hit me and kick me. Although they were told off by the teachers that didn't stop them and they continued whenever the teacher wasn't looking. One boy in particular bullied me a lot more than the others because before I had joined the school he was the smartest kid in his class. He got really annoyed if I completed something first. The school noticed that I was really good at Maths but they told me they weren't sure what to do so they gave me an advanced key stage 2 textbook to work on. There was only one copy of this book so I had to share it with another student who complained because I was ahead of him in the book and we had to keep flicking the pages back and forward and it was really distracting. Even though they gave me this extra book school was extremely boring and I was always distracted and looking out the window. I used to be really interested in school but every time I asked a question the teachers wouldn't answer me because they said it wasn't part of the lesson. I kept getting told off for misbehaving but I couldn't help it because I was bored and wanted people to like me so I was being silly and babyish on purpose. At the end of year 5 report I was given praise by the school for my work but I was extremely bored and depressed throughout the year.

During year 6 nothing much changed. I was given extra material to do but I still found it easy and I was still bored throughout the year. People in school kept teasing me and hitting me because I kept getting the Maths questions right but I didn't know why. In year 6 we were given a special Maths challenge run by the United Kingdom Mathematical Trust, which I found more interesting and slightly harder than the mathematics I was doing at the time. The results for that test weren't in the form of a mark, but instead those with a higher score got a certificate coloured either bronze, silver or gold and I was one of the few people who earned gold along with about five other students out of the entire year group. Although I was satisfied with the results from the Maths challenge I got bored very quickly once it was over.

Since it was still early in the school year the after school clubs hadn't started yet so there was still a chance to join one and sure enough there was one club that seemed right for me and that was chess club. In chess club I did well however I didn't advance in the ranks. The people at the top realised that if they didn't play anyone lower down the ladder then they couldn't lose their place. I kept being late into the club too because I find it hard to get organised and was always the last to get there and everyone else was already playing. I always ended up with the daughter of the teacher in charge of the club and although I always won I never got up in the ladder. About a month afterwards I started Karate which I found really fun and useful. Mum and Dad and my little sister started at the same time as me and we used to train together. After starting Karate I did actually think that it helped me to concentrate a bit more in school despite the fact I was extremely bored there because I was still doing the lower level Maths. After doing Karate for a bit the instructors helped me to stand up to the bullies. They told me that if you stand up to a bully you can stop them from hitting you just by talking and not being scared of them. When I did this it improved my self-confidence and I didn't have to use a single technique in primary school. Instead I just confidently told the bullies to back off from me and other people I knew.

Later in the year I was still bored and I only had three friends because every other boy made fun of me and called me names but I was starting to stand up for myself now. Mum and Dad went to meetings and the teachers usually said nothing too bad about me. I was still bored most of the time but at least I had chess club and Karate to keep me busy. As the year ended we had a chess tournament of the top eight players in terms of how many matches won, I came 1st. The school year ended and I was ready to move up to high school and I was hoping it would be better than primary. When the school reports went out I suddenly got a report saying how distracted I was in lessons and that I wasn't fulfilling my potential. I though that this meant that the school knew they could have done more to help me but didn't go to the bother of trying because now I was the local high schools problem.

When high school started I was still bored. I still had 2 of my friends there but the other students disliked me for the same reasons as in primary school and the bullying continued. I went from being one of the oldest people in the school to being one of the youngest and smallest and skinniest. I had hoped for high school to be better but it seemed just as bad until the CAT test which was a compulsory test for year 7's that assessed the students abilities and decided which set they would be put in for Science, English and Maths. The test was multiple choice and I found the Maths section very easy. During the two weeks between the test and the results I got to hate high school until one night I was sent home with a letter to my parents. I was really nervous what the letter would say and became more nervous when my parents read the letter asking them to come to school and meet the headmaster during parents evening. During the meeting I waited outside for a while until I was called over to the office where they were talking and the headmaster told me that I had got a really really high score in Maths and he showed me my CAT scores. After looking at the results I was really happy that as it turned out I was actually really good at something after all. I started to be happier now that I found what I was good at but I was still bored. In Maths class the teacher said that for homework's she would use a special website on which she would give us worksheets to do over the period of a few days and then the website would mark the answers for her. The teacher divided the class into 3 groups each group would have a different difficulty of homework based on the level system, the 3 groups were: 3 boosters (doing the worksheets that would help them reach level 3), 4 boosters and finally the 6 boosters which only me and 1 other person was in. The teacher said that if we wanted we could not only do the Maths she set for homework but also complete some of the other online worksheets. Over the next couple of weeks I completed all the 6 boosters and got 100% in all of them. The teacher was really impressed and she said if I wanted to I could have a go at the GCSE foundation material over the Christmas holidays. During the holidays I went along with the foundation GCSE material and got 100% in every worksheet so I thought to myself that since there was still about a week and a half of the Christmas holidays why don't I continue with the worksheets and move on to the higher GCSE material? When the Christmas holidays had ended I went to the teacher and told her that I had completed the entire GCSE material worksheets, she was astonished. A couple of days later my parents were asked if they could put me in for a mock GCSE exam. Although I didn't know at the time the school weren't sure if I had done the work myself or if someone else had done it for me. The mock paper was a little bit challenging and I was very nervous but when the results came in I was told that if that were a real paper I would have got an A. The results made me extremely happy and the school asked if I wanted to do the Maths GCSE course which I gladly accepted and got moved from my old Maths class into a GCSE class. Luckily for me I already knew a couple of the students from elsewhere who I met when my Dad did the sound engineering for an event. We were all geeky but otherwise we had nothing in common.

Word about me starting a Maths GCSE while still in year 7 went around the school very quickly and everyone in the school knew about a year 7 doing a Maths GCSE. However the one downside was that the bullies targeted me even more frequently, and although my Dad and the deputy headmaster told me how to deal with verbal bullying there was more than one occasion where it became physical. One time in the corridor me and the rest of my form group were waiting for the teacher when one of the other students began picking on me. I dealt with his verbal insults but then he tried to start a fight so I used what I was taught in Karate, if someone tries to start a fight: walk your way out of it, talk your way out of it then run your way out of it, however I couldn't walk or run because I was backed into a corner and talking my way out of it didn't work so the only option was to use Karate, he started hitting me with very rapid punches but before he hit my face I put my arms in the way and blocked his attack, while he was pummelling my arms I lifted my leg up and with one swift and well aimed kick I sent him wincing down the corridor clutching the shoe print on his trousers. One of the best parts was that people stopped picking on me, because about 5 other students saw me sent one of the toughest year 7's packing, and as one of the teachers later said "you should have hit him harder".

About a month or two after starting on the GCSE material I was finding it really easy and starting to get bored again. As a result the school asked me if I wanted to do an extra GCSE called Additional Maths which is an advanced version of the Maths GCSE which has lots of new stuff to learn at the same time as doing the normal GCSE which I gladly accepted. Unfortunately at this time me and my family had to move house for my Dads work and after searching my Dad chose a house in Acton, Wrexham so we started to pack our things. This meant that I would have to move schools in the middle of term. While we were moving I still continued preparing for the GCSE exams.

When the house moving had finished the GCSE exams were rapidly approaching but I needed a new school. The council said I should go to the nearest school but after visiting there for an interview we decided not to because it didn't have the services I needed. Because they didn't offer Maths at A-Level they wanted me to look at other GCSE's early but I didn't want to do this because Maths was what I was good at. The council insisted that I go to a local high school and if I did want to do my A level I should go to the local sixth form college part time. My Dad said I was too young for college and insisted that I instead should go to a school a few extra miles down the road because it had a sixth form so I could do the A level work once it started without being put in a class of 17 year olds. While I was waiting to take the GCSE exams I got bored and I started doing the work for my Maths A-Level. The GCSE exam was coming and the local newspaper found out that a 11 year old was taking two Maths GCSE's. I had been in a newspaper before as Prestatyn Carnival prince but this felt different. I was in about 3 newspapers before the exam came. About a week after I was in the newspaper my Dad got a phone call from a TV station asking if they could come and film me opening my results and my Dad said OK.

When it came time for the first GCSE exam I was incredibly nervous when I went in but I was really excited to be doing it. The exam was back in the Prestatyn high school even though I had moved schools so I was able to do some last minute revising on the car journey. I went into the hall and although this was extremely nerve wracking I thought the exam was really easy and I completed every question. A few days later the same thing happened with the second exam except I was even more nervous because the exam was supposed to be slightly harder since the course was more difficult but in the end I found it quite straightforward and was able to answer all the questions.

Once I had completed the GCSE exams I was able to work on the A-Level material. When it was time for the GCSE results, sure enough the press came but this time I was asked if I wanted to appear on the BBC evening news. I gladly accepted because I had always wanted to be on TV and I was shocked that I would actually get to fulfil my ambition. When it came to the results time me and my family went to Prestatyn. Mum stood next to me in front of the camera and Dad went and hid behind it because he didn't want to be on TV. Opening the envelope made me nervous but I was really pleased when I looked at the results and noticed that I got an A* in both exams. I was really happy and as a reward my parents took me out for the day and we went to a really nice sweet shop and got a huge bag of jelly beans and lots of other nice things.

I had passed my GCSE's and it was time to think about the A level. I had already started my new school and it was time to move onto year 8. Luckily this school had sixth form facilities and thus was able to provide me with some materials for me to do my AS and A levels there. I had done more than half of the A-Level material over the summer holidays and I really enjoyed it. The rest of the materials my parents got from a company in Glasgow called ICS. My Dad thought that if I was sent the stuff I could work at my own pace without having to rely on the school to teach me because I used to get bored waiting for other people to hurry up and answer the questions. The AS exams were approaching and I was getting nervous again and the local newspapers were back in contact. The day before the exam it was really bad weather and a lot of schools were closed because of the snow. I was really lucky that my school was one of the few that didn't close because of the weather. I had to do three exams for the AS Level and then I would have do to three more for A-Level. Mum and Dad persuaded me that I should do three at the start of the year and the rest during the summer because 6 exams would be too much to do in a week. Exam day came and I was nervous but I simply kept calm and carried on. I repeated this process for the other two exams. A few months later the results came in and I got an A in all 3 papers giving me an A overall.

I had to wait to be able to do the rest of the A-Level exams but I had already done the work. I started to get a bit bored again with the Maths work because it seems to me to be pretty easy. I had completed the material I needed to learn in about a couple of months but I had to wait until the school hosted the exams which was slightly annoying. I was a little bit nervous about doing the exams but I was really looking forward to doing them. But I was bored waiting for the A-Level exams so I asked my Dad if there were any more exams that I could do in Maths. My Dad spent ages looking at things with me and we looked at the Open University. I told my Dad I really wanted to do an Open University Maths course that was a bit more advanced and I found a course that focused on the history of Maths which sounded really interesting. I had to speak to a lady from the Open University on the phone because she wanted to make sure I was ready for it and would be able to cope with the work involved.

This course was only a really short course and it only took 10 weeks to finish. I was really happy because when I had finished it and had done well at it I was able to move on to a more difficult Open University course with lots more Maths to it. The first course that I did was a bit of a challenge sometimes because I had to write essays on the development of mathematics and I struggled to explain the information in ways other people could understand but I didn't know why.

The local newspapers kept coming back to me and I was flattered by all the attention. I also finally got to go on live radio which I liked but felt nervous about in case I made a mistake and lots of people would hear but the man who was Kryten in Red Dwarf was on first which was cool! This was the time of my A-Level and I was feeling extra nervous. The BBC news had come to film me opening the envelope and seeing what I got. Opening the envelope I could hardly bear to look but I breathed a sigh of relief when I looked and noticed that I had got an A.

About this time my Dad got contacted by a TV production company who were thinking about making a series about gifted children. We sat down and talked about it and I told my Dad I would really like to do it so we said yes.

The second Open University course ended soon after and when the results came in I was really happy to have passed. I got a really high mark in this course and I kept getting assignments back where I got more than 90%. For the next year I really wanted to do an astronomy course in addition to the next level Maths course. I ended up finding both courses not too difficult and luckily for me they weren't explanation orientated. I focused on the Maths and astronomy courses for a while. For the first time with the Open University I had to go to the local university and actually take a proper exam. Things were going well until I caught my fingers in a door and really injured them and I had to get an ambulance to take me to hospital where the doctors did an x-ray. My fingers were really really sore and I wasn't able to write at all. This meant that I couldn't write out the exam because they were wrapped up and strapped together. My Dad spoke to the Open University and they were really helpful and said if my Dad could sent them a letter from a doctor or a physiotherapist then they would be able to sort something out for me. We were able to get a letter sent in and I was told that I could dictate the exam to someone from the Open University and she would write it out for me. Exam day came and I was nervous as always but I went on with it. The exam went well and I felt good about the results though a little nervous.

Later on in the year I came home and got the opportunity to meet some people that my Dad had been speaking to about the TV Documentary. They wanted to interview me to see if they wanted me to be a part of it and how I would feel about doing it. After the interview they left and a few weeks later they phoned up and confirmed that they definitely wanted to do a documentary about me and my family. We agreed to do it and then they said that it was going to be a one-off documentary about just me and my family because I think they weren't able to find anyone else that they thought were suitable for the programme. I was really happy that I was going to be in a one-hour documentary and I couldn't wait for filming to start.

Meanwhile I started another OU Maths course and another OU astronomy course.

I kept having lots of problems in school and I had problems making friends. My parents had spoken to me about Aspergers in the past and lots of teachers that I had thought I had Aspergers too. We went to meet a doctor to see if he would refer me to a Psychologist to begin the assessments. A couple of assessments later and the TV crew tagged along and started the documentary filming. Although they weren't allowed to film the assessment they filmed me going in and out. The filming later began to occur most days and although it was a little annoying it was also very cool. Unfortunately in the middle of filming we found we had to move house again. We lived in a rented house and the owners of the house decided that they wanted to use the house for one of their family members. Because of this we had to find a new school for me. I wasn't worried about having to move schools because I had had a lot of problems with the school that I was at like getting bullied and I wanted to move school anyway. After moving house we tried a couple of schools until we found Darland high school and after checking it out we found that it was perfect because it had a specialised unit for people with communication issues.

About this time I started having problems with my astronomy course that I was doing because it began to ask for detailed explanation which I had problems giving. Filming continued and eventually the Asperger's diagnosis came in; we found I had Asperger's which was what me and my parents thought for a while. I was really pleased when they told me I had it because I was able to then read up about it and it explained a lot of things to me about the way I felt and the problems I had. It was really cool too that Issac Newton and Einstein had Aspergers too. I was lucky that when I started Darland I instantly made a friend. The TV cameras followed the first bit of my first day and watched me settle in. I found that *having TV cameras following me increased my popularity slightly.*

While we were making the TV programme the Director wanted me to go to Cambridge University to meet Professor Imre Leader who is the Cambridge head of Maths and also to meet Professor Simon Baron-Cohen who is the worlds Asperger's expert. I had a long chat with both professors and learnt a bit, although Professor Baron-Cohen wasn't included in the final version but Professor Leader was. We discussed about going beyond textbook mathematics and truly exploring the subject, he gave me a fun Maths puzzle and Cambridge looked like an amazing academic place.

Later on in the year I went to the Open University Office in Cardiff because I was having a bit of trouble explaining the mathematics. I was getting really upset because I was getting the right answers but my tutors weren't happy with the way I was explaining where I got my answers from. I got to meet my OU Maths tutor Angie Shier-Jones in person and discuss with her how to explain the mathematics. I was pleased that some of the other students had been having some problems explaining properly too.

I had settled in to Darland and things were going well. I went to a Birmingham games convention with a friend and the TV crew tagged along. Then as the school year was ending Professor Leader came round to talk to me at my house and he talked about Maths challenges and Maths camps and my options for the future and his suggestions were interesting and definitely something to think about. I was really excited that year about Maths camps and wanted to go on one. Later year 9 ended and then came my fourteenth birthday party with all of my friends and even my grandparents and the TV crew filmed that as well.

Over the holidays I studied a lot and soon it was time to start year 10 and the courses for the rest of my GCSEs. I had chosen separate science, food and systems because I thought they would be fun. I was bullied a bit still but the school did try to apprehend the bullies and they were really good at stopping any problems quickly, and I was really nervous about the documentary which would show soon. I got a preview of the programme when the Producer and the Director came round to show me. I was ok until a TV listings magazine said that I was going to be crying and some people teased me about it.

The exams for my OU studies were approaching and I was studying really hard to prepare. I found the exams to be a challenge because there was a decent length requirement for explanations but I reckon I achieved what I wanted however I am extremely nervous about it especially considering my difficulty with explanations. I am still waiting for the results.

[Since this was written the results have been received. Cameron successfully passed both courses.]

While I was waiting for the documentary to be shown my OU courses for the year finished and I started a photography course. I was really interested to learn how cameras work and how to take good pictures. The photography course was also an OU course so it would count as a short course towards my degree.

[Cameron has since completed the photography course and has successfully completed it, adding another 10 points towards his degree.]

The documentary came out and I was so nervous I couldn't sleep because I had got really upset one day and it was recorded by the camera and put into the programme. I was really worried that I would be made fun of because of it and I was nervous about what people would say, like calling me a wimp or a crybaby. However the comments received were surprisingly nice and I got lots and lots of them with over 1000 after a few days. When I went to school the day after the other students were treating me like a celebrity asking for autographs so I drew smiley faces and wrote funny things onto arms. Even at the local shop I was congratulated for my success by the nice ladies who work there. Over the course of two nights my list of Facebook friends went from fifty to about 350. In the future I hope to make even more friends and complete my degree.

12 Friends and Family

When one sibling is identified as gifted or talented and another is not, families need to be able to not just recognise the ability of the gifted child but to be just as clear on the necessity of recognising the abilities shown by the other children in the family. There is automatically a danger that the activity that is generated around a gifted child will make their siblings feel left out.

There are three principle risks with a gifted child with siblings. Firstly that the awards, certificates and the resulting praise will cause the siblings to get jealous of the attention that is being received, not just from their parents, but also from others including extended family and friends and school staff. Therefore there has to equal celebration for their achievements as well.

Secondly that the other children start to resent the amount of time that is spent on the gifted child. A gifted child may have tuition or training sessions to be transported to, need space and/or peace and quiet to practise or study or have competitions or games where not only do they have to go but so do other family members to offer support. There may well be time spent on meetings with teachers or coaches and researching new resources for the gifted sibling. It is important to make sure that any interests the other children may have are catered for and that the time, spaces and resources needed for these are provided. In any household there has to be organisation of priorities with choices and comparisons made, but probably the worst thing that could happen is that the gifted child's interests are always put first. Not only will other children resent this but the gifted child will have a distorted view of their own importance, which won't do them any favours socially in other situations.

Thirdly with the best will in the world there are only so many hours in the day and when there is more than one child with different requirements then priorities have to be set over which item is sorted out first. When we moved house to Wrexham we had 3 schools to pick for 3 very different children and had to start somewhere. In those circumstances we organised our enquiries in the order of Emma, our disabled daughter needing a Special Education school first, Cameron with his need for A-Level provision, as well as his 2nd year of high school education came second, and finally Bethany with her junior primary school needs. We didn't have to like it, but that is the way it worked out because of how difficult the first two were to arrange. We made sure that we sat Bethany down and explained why it was more complicated for the other two but that didn't make them more important and that we would be just as careful when we chose her school, she just had more options available.

Especially given our situation, with 2 children with Special Needs, one of whom is gifted, it is vital to make sure that each child gets time to themselves with each parent. Children need time when they are the centre of attention, doing whatever they want to do as an individual, which in our house can vary from playing World of Warcraft together for Cameron, to buying collectable rabbits at Antiques Fairs and shops with Bethany to endless games of "This Little Piggy" and rough-housing with Emma!

Whilst care needs to be taken with all siblings to ensure proper development of confidence and self-esteem, every child need not share the same experiences. Indeed sometimes families make the mistake of promoting activities that would benefit their gifted child but that would be of no interest to or beyond the capability of other siblings. The converse of course may also be true that families promote activities towards the "non-gifted" sibling that is of little interest to the gifted child, perhaps because they don't relate to or understand what the gifted child actually needs. This means that family activities have to be balanced so that everyone enjoys themselves; however there may need to be separate activities provided on occasions. Of course this balancing act of trying to make sure everyone is happy is something any family has to do on outings.

Studies have been undertaken which looked at the siblings of gifted children and found that no long term ill effects (outside of typical sibling difficulties that may occur) were observed in families where one child is labelled as gifted. One study published in 1999 went as far as arguing that it is advantageous to be the brother or sister of a gifted child. The report concluded that having an older gifted sibling was associated with less anxiety, better behaviour, social competence, and fewer behavioural problems.

The advice given by this study is mostly common sense:

- Parents should expect, and try to ensure that, their children do get along and learn mutual respect for each other and their abilities

- Teach children that being "fair" to all concerned does not always mean treating them "the same" as they are individuals with different wants and needs

- Ensure quality time with each child on a one to one basis showing interest in their own individual interests

- Appreciate each child for who they are and for their own abilities. Never compare them, for example "why couldn't you be more like your brother?", which is unfair to both children involved and will only cause resentment

- Ensure that one child is not made to feel (whether this may be true or perceived) that they are favoured over another

Clearly families with one or more gifted children with non-gifted siblings will face unique problems but equally they will also have unique assets. The achievements of the gifted child can be a source of celebration and pride for the whole family, if handled correctly. It can be inspiring for other siblings to see what can be achieved and encourage them to find their own talents in life and make the most of their own potential, whether they are gifted or not. It can help encourage development of self-discipline and teach about the need to put effort into any area that they want to do well in.

It is important to not show any bias towards any of the abilities of the children, for example favouring cognitive and academic abilities and not recognising other, less quantifiable talents. Clearly not every child reaches the level of ability required to be considered as "gifted" but the fact of the matter is that every child will have one or more areas of interest that require development and nurturing. We knew a child whose older brother was gifted academically, however this boy wasn't. Ironically the non-academic child was perfectly accepting of the situation and was happy with who he was and what his limitations were. However the boy's parents couldn't accept that one of their children wasn't particularly successful academically and insisted that before exams he was tutored for long hours to try and get him the same results that his brother had received. All that happened was that the child was miserable and missed out on a lot of other things he could have been doing in the year running up to the exams and after all that effort he still didn't do well! It was a perfect illustration of how hard work isn't enough to guarantee success if there is no talent to build on. We can only hope that at some point they noticed, and acknowledged, whatever direction his abilities did lie in.

Having a gifted child can be a great source of pride to parents; however caution must be used when dealing with siblings to ensure such pride doesn't create resentment or feelings of inferiority. Children have to be treated as individuals, with their own personal needs catered for, at the same time as being treated as equals in how they are loved and the amount of time and praise they get! To do anything else can create issues with both parties' self-esteem as the gifted child will develop an inflated sense of their own importance. We knew a family for a number of years whose son was talented in a number of athletic areas. When we first met them he was a pleasant, hard-working, modest young man and his parents were understandably proud of his achievements. However as time passed his parents started making unflattering and unfair comparisons between his performance and that of his peers. The arrogant attitude of his parents gradually spread to the child to the point where he refused to even join in a round of applause for others' success, refused to join in training activities if he didn't feel like it and was rude and dismissive of the other children. In a few years his personality had dramatically changed and the other children started avoiding him because nobody wants to be around someone who is rude to them! Finally his parents turned up with an older child one day and everyone was astonished to find that this was his sister because they had never mentioned her! She had become invisible while her brother's belief in his own abilities had become increased to the point where it had damaged his social development and that of his gift.

An interesting study at Cornell in 1984 found a tendency in families for mothers to identify their child as gifted but that their fathers did not, which can become a cause of marital conflict. The reason for this was simple; men tend to associate giftedness with a tangible measure of achievement whereas women tend to view giftedness alongside early developmental milestones. This is unfortunate as really children need support from both parents and the earlier that gifts are recognised, the better the chance of them being properly developed. Of course in an ideal world every parent would think that their children were special in their own way!

We have presented Cameron's perspective on the events in his life in the previous chapter. As this chapter is about the effect the life of a gifted child has on those close to them, Cameron's sister Bethany has put her thoughts down on paper.

I first found out that my brother was extremely good at Maths when I was 7 years old. My parents for a while thought that Cameron was really good at Mathematics but no school did anything about it until Cameron went to high school then the school started doing something about it by giving him some harder Maths. I found out that Cameron was a genius when my dad told me after Cameron came back from a meeting with his school. It was thrilling to hear that when Cameron went to school on Monday he was given super hard Maths and Cameron found that challenging. From then on I felt that my life was slowly starting to change because my life was starting to not be so normal. Then Cameron started to do Maths on the computer and later took a GCSE Mathematics mock paper and got an A. I was happy to hear that Cameron got an A. To me Cameron's Maths looks confusing but to Cameron the Maths is easy.

Cameron had to start doing intensive Mathematics for a big GCSE exam at the end of the school year. I was glad that I didn't have a big exam because I hate exams and I hate tests. Then was the big exam and I was really worried when Cameron was in the exam because I didn't know what he would get and how he would cope with it. Then my life really started to change because newspaper people started doing interviews with me and my family again. They had already done some articles before the exams but now there was even more. Two months down the line Cameron got his results and they were filmed on television for the news. The results were A* in Mathematics and additional Mathematics. My thought about TV cameras was keep that thing away from me! I didn't want to be seen on TV because I'd freeze and I wouldn't know what to say. Cameron didn't freeze on camera and knew what to say.

Then we started moving house because of Dads work it was stressful moving house from Prestatyn to Wrexham and it was hard work. I didn't like moving house because I liked the house we were in and I liked the school I was in a lot. It took a couple of months for the stressful move to finally be over and done with. We had a lot of help to move everything out of Prestatyn and into Wrexham. It was very hard to find schools for Cameron and for my sister Emma because Cameron needed an academic school and Emma needed a special school. We found me a school first called Acton Park! I liked it at Acton Park. Then Emma started going to St Christopher's then Cameron went to the Maelor in Penley. Meanwhile Cameron had finished the A-level material and was doing a different type of Mathematics with the Open University while he waited for the exams.

In January Cameron had to do 3 big exams and all of that was very stressful. How many big exams do you have to do in high school? It seems like a billion to me it's like Cameron's always studying for an exam I'd hate to be in high school. Afterwards Cameron was on the news to ask him how he felt. Then later on in July he went on to do another 3 big exams. More exams he's done a million already. Then about a month later the results were in and a TV crew came and filmed him getting 3 As. During the summer holidays Cameron went on with the OU material, I felt bored sometimes because when I wanted to play with Cameron he was almost always doing Mathematics or playing computer games. One day I came home to find 2 people standing in the hall filming Cameron. Then they started asking questions about school and Karate and asking if we wanted to do a documentary series on gifted children along with other child geniuses. I wasn't sure what to say other than yes. I was shocked to get asked so many questions and the fact that a giant camera was facing me. Why does the camera need to be so big?

Soon Cameron stupidly got his fingers trapped in a door and damaged his fingers which must have really hurt. His fingers were wrapped up for a few weeks and he couldn't write properly but the big problem was that his OU exam was a few days away. I was shocked to find Cameron had nearly broken his fingers I really didn't expect to see that when I came home from school. Luckily dad rang a physiotherapist called Gary and he gave Cameron a note saying that he had almost broke his fingers so he couldn't write the exam. A few days later a woman came round to the house, it was a Mathematics tutor and for the next 3 hours Cameron told the woman what to write for the answers. Soon after a TV crew appeared and began filming for the documentary, they were asking everybody in the family questions. At first I kept away from the the camera and I kept away from the TV crew but after a while I got used to it.

Cameron started struggling with Astronomy and it was getting really hard for him and soon we were told we had to move house I was sad to have to leave the house and my 3 friends. Moving was hard but not as hard as moving from Prestatyn to Wrexham and my Uncle came over and helped which made things a lot easier. Meanwhile Mum and Dad were trying to find Cameron a school which was difficult because we had to find a school with an Asperger's department while I settled in to St. Peters. Eventually my parents found Cameron a school called Darland and he went there because it had a really good communications unit. My sister Emma still went to St. Christopher's because Emma gets picked up in the morning. Meanwhile Cameron was setting in to Darland. After that Cameron and Mum went to Cambridge University to see Professor Leader who is an excellent Mathematician and Professor Simon Baron Cohen the world Asperger's expert. I was happy for Cameron because he got to meet these famous people but I had never ever heard of them.

Soon after Cameron and his friend Jonathan went to a game expo. I felt happy for Cameron because he was getting social interaction with a friend. Cameron had my phone because his wasn't charged because he forgot but it must have looked funny a teenage boy carrying round a pink phone! The summer holidays came and Cameron was studying a lot for the exams at the end of the course but I wished Cameron would go outside and enjoy the fresh air and play a game of tag. Also during the summer holidays the documentary filming ended. The summer holidays seemed to be flying by and then they were all over. Soon after school started back Cameron had 2 big exams in Maths and Astronomy. When Cameron was in the exam I was worried because I didn't know if he was going to pass or not although I thought he would. Soon after that Cameron started doing a Photography course.

Then the documentary came out on BBC3 it was thrilling to see all the family on TV. The documentary affected both mine and Cameron's school lives because everyone recognised us from the TV and both of us became more popular in school. I thought I looked silly on TV but people in my school thought I was funny.

Like Cameron I'm good at Maths but I am not as good as he is and Maths is not my favourite because my favourite subject is art. My second favourite subject is Sports and then Maths. Cameron hates sports and especially hates art. As well as having different opinions on subjects we also have similar opinions on subjects like we both dislike Welsh. I dislike Welsh because I don't like learning different languages but I'm good at Welsh I know because I was picked to be filmed for a programme on Welsh teaching as well as some other kids. I got filmed a lot as well as my partner I was nervous but I think I did fine.

I really enjoy doing my Karate even more than Cameron does and before Christmas I got invited to take my black belt. I was really nervous and it was really exciting and really hard work and it took 4 hours but I passed and I now have a black belt in Karate with my name on it in Japanese. I was really pleased and I took my belt into school to show all my friends.

13 In Closing

It's been said repeatedly throughout this book but it is more than worthwhile to say it again in closing - no 2 children are the same and as such hard and fast rules cannot be made. Children are individuals, whether they have been given a diagnostic label or have been found to have any special talent or giftedness. This doesn't mean that they can or should be treated like every other child with that diagnosis or like every other child with that same talent or gift! Decisions should be made based on a full knowledge of the child and their strengths and weaknesses and not on a generic "expert opinion". As much as the opinion of those within education and other associated professions is essential, it is worth bearing in mind that they aren't gods (although we have met a few in our time who appeared to think differently!).

There is no such thing as a "one size fits all" policy with human beings! There may be a limited number of responses to a situation but any action taken has to be for what the circumstances actually are, not what they should be. Emma suffered from a lack of progress in her schooling for a number of years. We can only speculate but her progress suddenly accelerated when she moved to St Christopher's School, which she still attends, who from her first day tailored her education to the little girl they had in front of them as opposed to the child described in her paperwork. The first thing they noticed, to their polite surprise, from our initial meeting onwards was that the behaviour they observed from her and what we described as her defining characteristics matched but that neither of those resembled what her diagnosis and notes, written by educational experts, said! Certainly what can't be denied is that she achieved targets in months there that had eluded others for a couple of years! Part of the reason this worked though was because we knew Emma so well and treated her, both then and now, as the person she is, not who we might want her to be.

As much as it can be painful at times it really doesn't do anyone any favours to ignore evidence of a child's abilities, strengths or weaknesses. As Einstein said, "If you judge a fish by its ability to climb a tree, it will live its whole life believing that it is stupid"; there is nothing to be gained by trying to get any child to measure up to what others feel their abilities should be, as opposed to what they are, apart from heartache.

The best thing that can be done is to only form opinions based on observations that come from being the parents, who are around them all the time, and who are not being afraid to change their opinion totally if proved wrong, or if the circumstances change. We would freely admit that we have changed the "plan of action" with Cameron several times, despite it being far from convenient for us, because something didn't work or no longer suited him. Everyone has met parents at some time who are so totally blind to the reality of their children that it can be breathtaking; those parents who say, "Oh, he didn't mean to be naughty!", while those round them are wondering if they're talking about the same child! It is a sad fact that we often met teachers who seemed surprised that we were clued in to what Cameron and Emma are really like.

It isn't easy being the parents of a gifted child, more so if the child has Asperger's Syndrome, and there will inevitably be times of despair and frustration but the simple fact of the matter is that our children deserve all the opportunities we can find for them and deserve the chance to be able to fulfil their potential. This can involve having to do most of the work yourselves in finding alternatives to the offered courses of action and establishing exactly what the legal responsibilities are of others to make provision and what the legal rights of the child are. Unfortunately these opportunities are few and far between in a system designed around the needs of the many, and often we need to create and fight for what these children want, need and deserve. There have been more than a few times where we have ended up rejecting what was put to us and inventing our own third option; for example bringing the notion of distance learning to supplement mainstream education doesn't seem to have ever been considered in the past. Parents who can't find an education system that provides what their child needs must hope for the next best thing; to find their child surrounded by those who are willing to admit that there is a need, who are prepared and are willing to accommodate any solution that the child's parents can create. Even better is when they are actively helpful.

When we made the BBC documentary "The Growing Pains of a Teenage Genius", we felt is was important for us to open our lives to the viewing public and show people a different side to giftedness; to let people see that there isn't a stereotypical "pushy parent" behind every gifted child! There have been a number of TV programmes made about children whose parents are frantically driving their children to achieve as much as possible as quickly as possible with little regard for what their child actually wants. The production company therefore had seen the need for a series of programmes to tell the stories of the naturally gifted, whose parents were providing them with the opportunities, but not driving the pace. They contacted parents that they could find and did a number of short test films. After these it was decided to reduce the number of participants to just our family. We suspect there were a number of reasons, partly based on our subsequent experiences, not least of which is that there appears to be among parents of children in accelerated learning, a reluctance to let them explain themselves, almost a belief that their parents should always do their talking for them! They were also looking for articulate children, which certainly fits Cameron, but perhaps a large part of the problem was finding others like us where the pace is set by the child themselves. That is not to say that they don't exist, but that they are frequently invisible, unwilling to talk in public about their experiences in case they expose themselves to harsh judgements and find themselves caught up in the condemnation of those who value speed above all else.

Our hope for the programme was to show the real Cameron Thompson - a wonderful boy with a passion for mathematics who pushes himself to succeed whilst desperately trying to be popular. Many people seem to think that gifted children choose to be different, little realising that it is not a choice any more than being born with blue eyes is a choice. The choice is what, if anything, is done about it, but it doesn't change the fact that he has this ability, whether it is ignored or developed. There is a perception that if he just stopped the Maths work, grabbed a football and started playing that the social fairy would just wave her magic wand and behold! Suddenly he would be "normal", whatever that actually means. This is a radically simplistic view of the whole situation and shows little grasp of the realities. After all, when he was in primary school his gift was being ignored by his teachers and he blended in even less then than he does now. His disruptive behaviour, his boredom and his gradual disillusionment were the results of little action being taken, none of which exactly made him fit in better! He didn't have a large social circle or suddenly develop a burning need to join in the football. A gifted child is what Cameron is and nothing will change that fact. The only thing that can be changed is what is done about it.

We have had much feedback from the programme, many hundreds of messages, and we can honestly say only a handful were in any way negative, an example being the opinion in the previous paragraph. The vast majority found the programme to be interesting, insightful, touching and inspirational and we therefore consider that we have been successful in what we set out to do. Sadly it continues to be abundantly clear that there are many "Camerons" out there who have the ability to succeed but not the opportunities. We have heard of children whose parents had been told that there was nothing to be done, that it could be damaging to do anything and left feeling that they were the only people in that position, not knowing where to turn. We have been sent personal emails from those who wanted to wish Cameron all the best and just to encourage him but also from those in similar positions who wanted to talk to someone who had, "Been there, done that" either for advice or just to talk to someone who understands.

Even though the primary focus was Cameron's gift for Maths there was also, by necessity, a considerable focus in the programme on his Asperger's Syndrome. This also resulted in a large response. We were contacted even before the programme actually aired by parents of children with Asperger's who said that their child was excited at the prospect of seeing a child like them on TV. After the programme there were responses both from people whose response was relief, either theirs or their child's, to seeing another child with just the same issues with their Asperger's as Cameron and from those with Asperger's, in their early 20's, who wanted to reassure Cameron that as time passed the social difficulties lessen. We also received emails from parents of children undergoing the Asperger's Syndrome diagnostic process who were given hope that, should the result be positive for Asperger's, that it really wasn't the end of the world. It may also help to alter people's perceptions of how Asperger's presents, showing someone who is different from the stereotypical Asperger's child, including views held by those in the teaching profession.

We also hope that people will remember the programme, even if it has no current personal relevance, in the future should their own, or children they are acquainted with be in a similar situation. We would also hope that it will have some effect on education even if only that teachers will keep his situation in mind when they encounter a child who appears to be at the upper end of the spectrum of gifted. We can only hope that maybe it will contribute to changing the view within the educational establishment that all parents whose children are usually high achievers are forcing their children down this path, at the expense of allowing natural childhood development.

Gifted children need their families, their schools, and society as a whole to have a realistic idea of what being a gifted child is and is not. On the whole the experts do seen to agree on one thing; when a child has a clear gifting it cannot and should not be ignored. Ignoring it will not benefit the child, which means that decisions have to be made on what action to take. Quite what should be done is where the opinions differ!

What To Do If Your Child May Be Gifted

After reading this book you may have found yourself thinking that your child may be gifted and wondering where to go next. First and foremost the most important thing is to truly know your child. Step back from the situation and try to observe them, as impartially as it is possible when it comes to your own children. Judge your child against a list of qualities that are found in gifted children, like the one provided by the National Association of Gifted Children. If your child is gifted then they should have many of the listed traits. Not being gifted should never be judged as a failure; there is absolutely no failure in a child being highly intelligent as opposed to gifted. We would hope that if one thing has come through loud and clear in this book, it is that little good is to be achieved from trying to push a child into becoming something they're not. In fact there is the opportunity to do a lot of harm, as well as running the risk of missing the potential that they do actually possess.

If you still suspect that they may be gifted, sit your child down and speak to them about how they feel in school. Ask them how they find the work they are doing; understand what is expected of them by their teachers and what they expect of themselves. In the UK the National Association of Gifted Children offers a telephone helpline to parents who are unsure of where to turn and what to do next, and many parents have found them to be an absolutely invaluable help both in terms of getting advice and of just having someone to talk to that understands the needs of gifted children. Depending on where you are in the UK you may be able to hook up with one of their regional branches and join in one of their events. These events are often not just for parents but are designed for the child as well and offer an excellent chance for both you and your child to talk to someone who understands, and shares, many of the same challenges and experiences.

Secondly, even with the problems that we have had in the past with some of Cameron's schools, we still believe that speaking to your child's school is an essential first step. It may well be that you will end up dissatisfied with their response but at least give them the opportunity! Most schools nowadays have a member of staff with a responsibility for organising the provision for those children who are Gifted & Talented / More Able & Talented, or whatever term is favoured in your area, and it may be that you can meet with them. Be prepared when you meet to give plenty of well reasoned examples of why you feel your child may be gifted; remember that teachers typically deal with dozens of pupils each year in a very narrow setting and therefore don't necessarily get to know their students that in depth. It helps to have done some research beforehand and to have your points ready and to hand in a short list. However the operative word here is short! A list, and any supporting research, isn't an opportunity to try and beat them into submission! If you have brought anything more than a short list of points be prepared to leave the information for the school to look over at their convenience.

Do remember that on the whole teachers and schools want to help your child in every way they possibly can. Charging in all guns blazing demanding things be done is of no benefit to anyone. For one, the natural human reaction to being attacked is to automatically go on the defensive. The whole point of a meeting about your believing your child might be gifted is to request that their teachers take a harder look at them and perhaps view them in a new light. Forcing them to entrench and defend their current position on your child is completely counter-productive! One other point is that the teaching staff are all too familiar with aggressive parents pushing children forward without any valid cause, rather being driven to prove that their little darling is better than everybody else's child and unable to accept anything less. Childhood is not, and never will be, a race; there is no prize for first past the post! It is important to make sure that teachers know and understand that yours' is a genuine concern, based on what you feel is actually in your child's best interests, and is what your child would want.

If you are asking the question and your child hasn't even started school yet then it may be better to pause and let you, your child and their teacher, catch their breath and see how they settle into school first. This also gives their teacher a chance to get to know your child and to get a better idea of what their strengths and weaknesses are. By all means talk to the nursery school teacher, or whoever is responsible for their education, about your thoughts and feelings but don't expect miracles at this stage. Many children, including your own, have to learn the skills of sitting relatively still in a classroom and working with other pupils with whom they have to share the teacher's attention and time. It will take a couple of months for them to all settle in.

Give the school the opportunity to get back to you. After all if they haven't considered it at all previously then all the relevant staff need to examine the information you have presented. It can take weeks to get a response sometimes, which isn't an unreasonable amount of time when you consider the number of people that may need to be spoken to and give their input. When they get back to you, listen to what they have to say, even though you may not agree with it. Many parents want to believe their child has some form of special talent that sets them aside from their peers but more often than not that is simply not the case. Allow the school to present their justifications for their conclusion and show them enough respect to consider their reply properly, as they did for your opinion.

This all rather assumes that what you were greeted with wasn't a knee jerk rejection! It is sadly more than possible that your child's teachers will refuse to contemplate the idea that your child is gifted. There are a number of different ways to react to this. Response partly depends on whether they bothered to think about the issue, or if you even had a chance to present your case. If the school refused to even do you the courtesy of taking the time to consider it, then it is clear that you will not see eye-to-eye on this, and it is time to look at other options for assistance. If on the other hand you were rejected but only after careful consideration, then it is worth while checking the basis for your belief. It may be worth getting confirmation of their ability from an outside source of some sort, preferably one that has nothing to gain from stating that your child is gifted! In our case we asked a Maths tutor friend to check Cameron's ability before we went and asked the school if there was anything more they could do for him.

If you end up going down a more formalised route, for example with an Education Psychologist, be prepared for either a long wait to see them or expect to pay and go privately. The problem with getting a private assessment to speed up the process is that the school may be unwilling to follow its' advice. There can be a number of reasons for this, principally the school may believe that the findings are fundamentally flawed, maybe even on the basis that someone who is being paid to find out if a child is gifted will therefore find that they are, regardless of what the reality actually is. The second problem can be that a recommended course of action from a private educational psychologist may be completely impractical for a school to implement when they have a classroom worth of children for whom to make provision. It may also make suggestions of what needs to be provided with no ideas on how actually to offer it.

In parts of the UK it has not been unheard of to wait nearly 12 months for an Educational Psychologist's assessment. If the question of giftedness is being considered alongside other concerns such as Asperger's Syndrome that wait can be much longer – even as much as two years. This even assumes that, firstly you were able to find someone willing to refer your child, as generally parental referral isn't accepted, secondly that the professional who refers your child doesn't manage to refer them to the wrong team or list, so that you wait for months before finding out, and then have to start all over again and thirdly that you won't find your application and referral for an assessment rejected! In case this is viewed as overly cynical we should state at this point that Cameron has had the second situation happen at least twice and the third one once! We were informed that Cameron didn't have special needs and therefore didn't need an assessment. This is despite the fact he was then 12 and studying for a

Maths degree, so what does it take to be "special"? To say nothing of the fact that his Asperger's Syndrome was generally accepted as fact at this point by most of the education professionals who dealt with him, we just wanted it to be formally confirmed.

Note that we stated that there is a risk that no one will refer your child but there is also the risk that they will be ejected from the waiting list. The first appointment they get before assessment can be a sort of "gate keeper" appointment where a professional has to be convinced that there is an issue to examined before your child even gets onto the waiting list proper!

Even when the appointment does come around you should not expect instant answers; usually more than one session is required to be able to do a thorough evaluation and they may want to involve other branches of the medical profession, for example physiotherapy, before producing a report. Between waiting lists to get appointments and then the time it takes for reports to be agreed upon and written, this process can take months on end.

One reason that may be given for refusal to perform an assessment is that many Education Psychologists actively discourage the testing of very young children. It is felt that the results they may obtain are unreliable, with the minimum age for reliable IQ testing judged to be 5 and that for most special needs conditions to be diagnosed they generally wait until the child is about 7. This is because before that point a child's concentration and behaviour aren't reliable enough to be sure they won't to create inaccurate results.

Whether or not there is a label of "gifted", it is imperative to make sure your child understands what it means for them, and where their strengths and weaknesses lie. Encourage your child to explore their strengths by giving them the opportunities to do so and not by forcing them into something they don't want to do. It is not unheard of for parents who upon being told their child may have an ear for music to automatically sign them up for piano and violin lessons 5 days a week without ever speaking to them first! If they are pushed in a direction they don't want to go then they may well come to resent it or abandon it at the first available opportunity. Children also need to feel that they are more than just a set of abilities, to know that they are still valued for who they are, all that is different is that they get to do some new activities. They also, as previously discussed, need to feel in control of their own lives, to learn how to deal with challenges and failure and finally how to be children and be allowed to grow up at their own pace!

We have always strived to make sure that all three of our children feel equally valued and loved, when they are all very different in their abilities and even in what it takes to make sure they know what they mean to us.

Don't leave everything to your child's school, at the same time as being careful that you don't tread all over their toes if it isn't necessary. It's much better to have a good relationship with your child's teacher than have them want to dive under their desk every time you approach! Find out what your child is doing at school and then support it at home. Read with them, help them with their homework and their school projects, go to their parents evenings, school concerts and the like. Be interested and encouraging parents, listening to all the stories they have to tell; from the details of how their day went, complete with ever-changing childhood friendships and loyalties, to what fascinating new facts they learnt that day to what their favourite new singer is! In other words, all the things that any child needs from their parents. Added to this a gifted child needs their parents to make sure that any unique needs that they have are being met. This means listening to everything they say, watching for cues that all is not well, that they are being pushed too hard or that they aren't being pushed hard enough.

One problem that can occur is that a school may agree that your child is gifted but then fail to do enough to provide for this. If it is simply that they don't have the resources needed, and they acknowledge this, then at least it is possible for you to go and try and find a solution. This has happened several times to us with Cameron and we found the schools concerned were generally pretty reasonable. The best way to manage these situations is to maintain open communication, so that everyone knows where they stand, and for all parties to keep in mind the other sides point of view and try to reach a compromise where necessary.

A slightly different problem is when a school isn't providing properly for a gifted child yet insists that they are! This was our problem during Cameron's latter years of primary school. This is harder to deal with than outright denial, but this is where a firm label can be your friend. A cast iron diagnosis carries with it certain duties and legal obligations. Sadly in the end the bull-in-a-china-shop approach may be the only course of action left; just try to choose your battles carefully but equally don't be afraid to fight for what your child needs to succeed and be happy.

Remember this in closing; "In the final analysis it is not what you do for your children but what you have taught them to do for themselves that will make them successful human beings" (Ann Landers).

Understand that gifted or not, labelled or not, your child is still the same person that you always knew and loved. The most important aspect to raising any child is to ensure that they develop into happy and successful adults and no label will ever change that.

-END-

Made in the USA
Charleston, SC
15 March 2012